Fred Astaire

Fred

YALE UNIVERSITY PRESS   NEW HAVEN & LONDON

Astaire

Joseph Epstein

Published with assistance from the foundation established
in memory of William McKean Brown.

Frontispiece: The best way to hear Fred Astaire sing is not with the
large orchestras that accompanied him in his movies, but in
something closer to a small-room or studio atmosphere.
Gene Lester/Hulton Archive/Getty Images

Set in Janson by Integrated Publishing Solutions.
Printed in the United States of America.

Library of Congress Cataloging-in-Publication Data
Epstein, Joseph, 1937–
Fred Astaire / Joseph Epstein.
p. cm.—(Icons of America)
Includes bibliographical references and index.
ISBN 978-0-300-11695-3 (cloth : alk. paper) 1. Astaire, Fred,
1899–1987. 2. Dancers—United States—Biography. I. Title
GV1785.A83E68 2008
792.802'8092—dc22
[B]
2008015512

A catalogue record for this book
is available from the British Library.

This paper meets the requirements of
ANSI/NISO Z39.48-1992 (Permanence of Paper).

10 9 8 7 6 5 4 3 2 1

For Mary and Jake Stein
Ginger and Fred without even having to
step onto the dance floor

Contents

Contents

Preface

Federico Fellini's 1986 movie *Ginger and Fred* is about Fellini's deep distaste for the pervasiveness, and concomitant vulgarity, of television in modern life. Very Felliniesque, it contains lots of gentle freaks, wonderful cityscapes, and many moments goofy, charming, and touching. In the movie, a television show called *We Proudly Present* books various oddballs—spiritualists, mystical clergymen, midget dance troupes, retired admirals, transvestites, a woman who breaks down after going a full month without watching television—who speak with an Italian Bert Parks–like master of ceremonies about their zany and pathetic lives.

Among the acts booked is a couple who thirty years

before used to make a living on stage impersonating Fred Astaire and Ginger Rogers. The Ginger impersonator is played by Fellini's wife, Giulietta Masina, the Fred Astaire impersonator by Marcello Mastroianni. In the movie, "Ginger" is still in decent repair, but "Fred" is on the edge of extinction: seedy, a heavy drinker, profane, with a harsh cigarette cough, easily winded, ready to pop off into death at any moment. Each has been paid eighty thousand lire to appear on *We Proudly Present*. But as the movie plays out, we discover that they are really there because of the longing of each to see the other once again.

Giulietta Masina's character is named Amelia Bonetti, Marcello Mastroianni's is Pippo Botticella. She is efficient, orderly, the brains and backbone of the act, though not without the sweet mischievousness that Signorina Masina so often brought to her art; he is anarchic, with strong political views, capable of all sorts of craziness, full of artistic temperament, the kind of Italian who has never had his arms in the sleeves of his coat but wears it always draped dramatically over his shoulders. At one point before they go on the show, he does a bit of toe tap, showing that with his feet he can imitate a train, a typewriter, a machine gun, while claiming that he can also do classical, modern, comic, romantic, and pastoral dances.

When their turn to appear on the television show arrives, they dance to a medley of Astaire songs: "Cheek to Cheek," "The Continental," "Dancing in the Dark." The dancing is not great but is somehow very moving, with a slight hint of menace about it that derives from the distinct possibility that Pippo could drop dead out of exhaustion right there on the stage. But as we watch it, especially the Fred Astaire part, we recognize that there is something faintly, perhaps more than faintly, ridiculous about these dances, the funny moves, especially those that Mastroianni makes with his arms. ("Put your arm down, Pippo," Amelia whispers to him as she guides him through their old routine.) And then we realize that there is something absurd, too, about a man in tails who does tap and ballroom dancing with a woman in a dress that makes sense only on stage. "I'm going to sneeze," Pippo says, "I have a feather [from her dress] up my nose." (The real Fred Astaire encountered a similar difficulty with one of Ginger Rogers's dresses while dancing to "Cheek to Cheek" in the movie *Top Hat*.)

Watching these two aging, magnificent Italian actors do their Fred and Ginger in this bittersweet movie makes us wonder why the originals, and especially Fred Astaire, were themselves so captivating. "When I was a boy," the middle-aged president of the television station in the movie says, "I spent hours in my room trying to imitate the sublime Fred Astaire." But then most men not completely brutes at one time or another have also tried to imitate Astaire. And a great many females, young girls to older women, have ardently wished to dance with him.

Now here is some good news: Fred Astaire, too, spent hours—and hours and hours and many more hours—trying to imitate Fred Astaire, if not in his own room then in movie studio rehearsal halls. What is more, he had little taste for social dancing; and though almost every woman he ever met socially longed to dance with him, most found him, when he could be dragged onto the floor at a social event at all, less than dazzling, even a bit uninterested. We cannot know what pleasure his dancing gave Fred Astaire—one assumes that it was the high delight that doing something blissfully well gives anyone able to operate at his level of mastery—but it can be said that he was less interested in dancing per se than in overall dance performance, at which, the world has long since come to agree, nobody ever did it better.

About Astaire's sublimity there seems to be little argument. Of what does this sublimity consist? Why does this far-from-traditionally-good-looking man singing these light songs while doing intricate and smooth steps in splendidly tailored clothes make so many men wish, however briefly, that they had been he, and so many women wish they had been his partner? Whence derived Fred Astaire's sublimity, his magic? That is the great, happy question at the center of this little book.

Fred Astaire

A good measure of the success behind the Astaire-Rogers
partnership is also owed to the fact that they came together at a time
when an extraordinary clutch of great songwriters were at work,
not least among them Irving Berlin, here at the piano.
© Bettmann/CORBIS

Like Kissing Your Sister

Astaire—something in the name suggests brilliance, dazzle. Astaire implies "a star"; so, too, a stairway, perhaps one leading to Paradise ("with a new step every day"); Astarte is also, the mythologies report, the name of a minor goddess, one of high and productive energy. The name Astaire enlivens even the otherwise somewhat stodgy name of Fred. "Ladies and Gentlemen, the Academy is proud to honor that greatest of all dancers, male or female, classical or modern, ballet or ballroom, rap or tap, break or flake, highbrow or low, Mr. Fred Astaire." Thunderous, nearly unrelenting applause follows.

In fact, Fred Astaire's name at birth—he was born on May 10, 1899—was Frederick Austerlitz, II. His father,

Frederic (without a k) I, known to family and friends as Fritz, was rather a bust. He had left the Austrian army in 1892 and, departing Vienna, came to the New World to strike it rich. He struck it, from most accounts, scarcely at all. After shoring up in Omaha, Nebraska, Fritz Austerlitz (the name rhymes in a way that suggests unseriousness) took a series of dead-end jobs: in the leather business, as a cook, as a drummer of fancy goods, and eventually as a salesman for a brewery. (His son claimed he prospered at this last job, though there is no strong evidence about whether this is true.) Not without charm, the twenty-seven-year-old Fritz Austerlitz met and in fairly short order made pregnant a seventeen-year-old girl named Johanna Geilus; no one seems to know the precise fate of the child of this early pregnancy, who must have died either in a miscarriage or at birth. Two years later the Austerlitzes had a daughter Adele, and two and a half years after that a son Frederick, Freddie, Fred (hold the Fritz), the subject of the slender disquisition now in your hands and, not at all by the way, by general consensus the world's greatest male ballroom and tap dancer.

Turn-of-the-century Omaha may have had its virtues, but the absence of snobbery evidently wasn't high among them. The Austerlitzes were nowhere near the top of such social heap as the city mounted. From Frederic père's shaky hold on his job, and from photographs of the family's modest house, they look to have been closer to lower middle class, with some danger of sliding a touch or two farther down the splintery pole of the early-twentieth-century American class system. The Austerlitzes appeared, in short, to be a family going no place fast.

The children, Adele and Fred, seemed normal and happy enough. They did decently in school; they enjoyed each other's companionship. Johanna decided to enroll Adele, who early showed promise of being a great beauty, in a local dancing class. Her younger brother was also enrolled. A bad moment came when Adele and Freddie lost out in a contest to be among the attendants for a king and queen parade put on by a local lodge called the Kings of Ak-Sar-Ben (Nebraska spelled backwards). They lost not for want of talent but because only the well heeled and well born, by the Omaha standard of the day, were picked. The experience gave Johanna Austerlitz an overpowering sense that her children's fortunes were best sought outside Omaha.

A modest woman, given to backing her children completely, though not bragging unduly about them, Johanna Austerlitz had the thought of grooming her beautiful daughter for a career as a dancer, with her son Freddie, at least at this point, going along for the ride. So when her daughter was not yet eight, her son still five, she herself twenty-six, she took them off to New York to attend dancing school and prepare for a living in show business. The radical plan was to leave her husband back in Nebraska, whence he would send money to keep the enterprise afloat, though it is unclear whether he was able to do so in a sustained way. One of Fred Astaire's biographers even claims that Fritz had a child with another woman in Nebraska, a second Mrs. Austerlitz, though Astaire, who always defended his father, held him up as a solid and good man.

The Austerlitzes (mère, soeur, et frère) arrived in New York knowing no one but the name of a dancing teacher given them by the children's dancing teacher in Omaha. They checked into a hotel near the dance studio at 23rd Street near Eighth Avenue. On the advice of their new dance teacher, the children's surname was changed to Astaire; the mother later dropped the *Joh* and became Anna Astaire, later Ann to friends. The director of the dance school, a man named Claude Alvienne, thought that Adele and Fred were talented, though he was not about to say for certain that they had a real future in show business. Ann in effect "home-schooled" her kids, except for a two-year lull in their career when they attended a regular school in New Jersey. If there was disharmony, or even sadness, among this brave little trio, it was never mentioned, then or later. Somehow or other they made their way.

Claude Alvienne worked up routines for Adele and Fred as a brother-and-sister act, and such an act they would remain until Adele's retirement in her early thirties. In one of their childhood numbers, Adele, then the taller of the two, played Cyrano to Fred's Roxanne. Alvienne arranged bookings at small fees for them at secondline New Jersey theaters. Soon enough they went on the road, where their bookings were neither plentiful nor hugely rewarding. They continued their dance education; in New York they lived in a small furnished apartment. Adele was the natural of the two children, all shimmering beauty and spontaneity, with great élan; Fred, who had to work harder at everything, took his dancing more seriously. Most theater managers who booked them considered Adele the one with the smashing career ahead of her.

Through practice and persistence they eventually connected with the Orpheum theatrical circuit, which sent them on the road for a fee of $150 a week plus expenses. A dance teacher and director named Ned Wayman wrote a new act for them, at the price of $1,000, payable in installments. In big-city theaters the glow of their performance was dimmed by such glamorous names on the same bill as Douglas Fairbanks, Sr. (later a friend of Fred's in Hollywood). They continued to work hard, to grind it out, appearing alongside animal acts, acrobats, and low comedians. It was onward and upward, but in what must have seemed excruciatingly slow motion.

Ann Austerlitz Astaire was a careful money manager, and she worked things out so that when they weren't touring, she and her children stayed at swank resorts. Social mobility, clearly, was part of the grand plan. As adolescents, Fred and Adele developed a taste for the good, even the high, life. At one such resort, a place called Water Gap House in Delaware Water Gap, Pennsylvania, Fred reports in his memoir, *Steps in Time*, he "first learned to play golf, swim, and ride." Boys took a powerful interest in Adele, who seemed to give off fumes of sexual promise the way Eula Varner, that luscious girl in Faulkner's *The Hamlet*, did—Eula who could transform anywhere she went, as Faulkner put it, into "a grove of Venus." Mary Pickford, shooting a film nearby, stayed at Water Gap House the second year the Astaires were there. Peter Arno, the *New Yorker* cartoonist, was another guest. The allure of the posh was not lost on the Astaire kids. By the time they were in their twenties, Fred and Adele would rate as pretty damn posh themselves.

They acquired a new dance teacher, a man named Aurelia Coccia, a veteran vaudeville performer who streamlined their act, getting rid of their old skits and turning Fred and Adele into a straight song-and-dance act. They revised and rehearsed, polished and honed, found fresh songs, altered and added new dances. They played New England, where Adele attracted the boys from Yale. Thinking Fred her older brother, the Yalies took him up, as a way to get to Adele.

The contrast between Fred and Adele showed up early in their career as a team. Along with being hardworking, a perfectionist, Fred was a worrier: worried above all about little screwups in performance that would get in the way of his modest but unrelenting ambition, which was, as he told Edward R. Murrow much later in his life, "to knock 'em in the aisles as often as I could."

Adele was beautiful, effortlessly talented, candid, one of those rare women who could be attractively coarse. She was the perennial live wire, highest possible altitude and voltage. From an early age she knew that men were interested in her, and she could tell you, with blatant precision, why. At seventeen she allowed that "I've already got quite used to people grabbing my fanny backstage— that is, when they weren't all homos." She didn't mind calling a stagehand "a stupid fucker," or asking someone she caught looking up her skirt whether he saw "the ace of spades." When her brother apologized for her raw frankness, she might add, "Why the fuck shouldn't I say what I feel?" One of the reasons that to this day some people think that Fred Astaire is Jewish is that during the 1930s, with Hitler in power, someone made an anti-Semitic remark about Adele's friend the actress Lilli Palmer, prompting Adele to tell the offender to take it back, and quickly, claiming that she herself was Jewish.

If Adele was utterly at ease with men, Fred was careful with women, and waited until his middle thirties to marry a woman who was not in show business and who had a four-year-old son. He adored her. Let the record show that he was always faithful to her despite what must have been endless opportunities. Adele, on the other hand, appears to have been stimulated by worthlessness in men. She is said to have lost her virginity to George Jean Nathan, the theater critic who was H. L. Mencken's partner on the *Smart Set*, a man many years older than she, and, from various accounts, far from an appetizing specimen. She later bedded Cecil Beaton, providing him a pause (evidently not one that much refreshed) in an otherwise largely gay life (though Beaton and Greta Garbo were often thought, in the phrase of the day, an item).

When Adele married at thirty-four, she chose an English nobleman, Charles Cavendish, the sixth child of the Duke of Devonshire, nine years younger than she and a dedicated drinker who pegged out with cirrhosis of the liver before he was forty. She was gutsy, Adele, gallant, amusing to be with, and generous in spirit. John Green, who later served as musical director of two Fred Astaire movies, *Easter Parade* and *Royal Wedding*, remembered Adele as "able to be pert without being precious; cute but never coy; hokey, when appropriate, but never corny; moving without being maudlin. She had an uncanny sense of the fine line between sentiment and sentimentality, was sexy but never vulgar, and always utterly beguiling." Noël Coward, who loathed falsity, adored Adele. Her spirit is nicely captured in a needlepoint cushion she made for her brother and sister-in-law: on one side there was a floral design, on the other the words "Fuck Off."

Fred was much tighter, in every way. Once married, he was a homebody. His wife was his dearest friend, and perhaps his only confidante. His politics were apparently Republican, though he never pushed them; politics bored him. He was churchgoing, religious in a way he never cared to speak about, though his religion was evidently important to him. But then he never made a big thing about any aspect of his personal life. He gave dull interviews, making journalists feel—who is to say wrongly?—that his private life was his business. He golfed, for God's sake, and in great earnest. As soon as he could afford them, he bought racehorses, and one of them, a horse named Triplicate, turned out to be a big money winner for him. But above all he put effort, relentless effort, into making his own vision about the art of the dance look perfectly effortless.

Without Adele as his partner at the beginning of his career, Fred Astaire might have ended up a suburban husband, selling swank high-line cars (for which he had a lifelong taste). In their early years as a dance team, Adele supplied the main excitement. But the commitment to perfection was not in her in the way that it was in her brother. "It was different for me," she is quoted saying in the Tim Satchell biography of Fred Astaire, "but show business and dancing and worrying were in my brother's blood—it was not just his work, it was his life." Endless hard work is more than a theme in Astaire's career; it was the reason his career ascended to the heights it did.

The dance team of Astaire and Astaire slowly rose on the marquees of the theaters they played, as did their fees, soon hitting $350 a week. This was the age of the impresario, of Abe Erlanger, Flo Ziegfeld, and the Brothers Shubert, with their revues and extravaganzas. The Astaires were bidden by the Shuberts to appear in *Over the Top*, a show originally called *The Nine O'Clock Revue* because of a plan to start half an hour after most theatrical performances in New York. This was it, Broadway, the big time. No smash, the show nonetheless did do decent business, in New York and afterward on the road. In his memoir Fred Astaire quotes the verdict of Louis Sherwin, the critic of the *New York Globe:* "One of the prettiest features of the show is the dancing of the two Astaires. The girl, a light, spritelike little creature, has really an exquisite floating style in her caperings, while the young man combines eccentric agility with humor." Not exactly "I greet you at the beginning of a great career," but a start.

The Astaires did another show for the Shuberts, *The Passing Show of 1918,* from which they garnered more praise. The journalist Heywood Broun, that human unmade bed, awarded them this gentle critical kiss: "In an evening in which there was an abundance of good dancing, Fred Astaire stood out. He and his partner, Adele Astaire, made the show pause early in the evening with a beautiful loose-limbed dance. It almost seemed as if the two young persons had been poured into the dance." *Poured into the dance* is a metaphor that, like Broun himself, could use a little pressing, but the praise comes through.

Once the Astaires arrived on Broadway, it really was onward and upward. They appeared on bills with such great names of the day as Al Jolson, Fanny Brice, and Charlie Ruggles. Their price went up to $550 a week, enough for Fred to think about acquiring a sports car. Alexander Woollcott, spelling their name wrong, noted that "there should be a half dozen special words for the vastly entertaining dances by the Adaires, in particular for that nimble and lack-a-daisical Adaire named Fred. He is one of those extraordinary persons whose sense of rhythm and humor have been all mixed up, whose very muscles of which he seems to have an extra supply, are facetious." Facetious muscles aren't easily visualized, but let that, too, pass. Hey, as long as they spell your name wrong!

By 1920 the Astaires were making $750 a week. They spent lots of their free time in smart nightclubs. A choreographer in a dud show they did called *The Love Letter* taught them a dance in which they ran around, shoulder to shoulder, as if on a six-day bicycle racetrack; it later came to be called the "Oompah Trot," and they used it over and over because it was an unfailing showstopper. When reviewers panned shows Adele and Fred were in, exceptions tended to be made for them. "When they dance," Robert Benchley wrote in *Life*, "everything seems brighter and their comedy alone would be good enough to carry them through even if they were to stop dancing (which God forbid!)." Now that is what real praise looks like.

Backstage one night in their dressing room appeared a brilliant young Englishman named Noël Coward, a contemporary who would become a lifelong friend and who suggested that the Astaires take their act to London, where they were certain to be a knockout. A young not yet fully fledged producer named Alex Aarons, whom Astaire met when Aarons was working at Sulka's, the men's shop noted for its robes and dazzling neckties, later pushed them to take his show *For Goodness Sake* to London, which they agreed to do. Their English success was instantaneous. "Your success here is assured," Coward told Adele. "You've got youth, energy, humor, looks, and fun. That's exactly what the English like." *Autre temps, autre moeurs;* as we have sadly come to learn, there wasn't always to be an England, at least not of the kind Noël Coward described.

Soon Fred Astaire—in his accent, his clothes, his general manner—came to appear mid-Atlantic, so strong did the English influence on him seem, while his sister married an Englishman and eventually became Lady Adele Cavendish. At one of the Astaires' early shows in England, Prince Albert—son of King George V and, at his brother Edward's abdication to marry the dour Mrs. Wallis Simpson, one day to be King George VI—turned up. He adored the Astaires and brought his friends and family to see them. He began inviting Fred and Adele out to dinner and parties after performances. The King of England is supposed to have said of the Astaires: "They seem a decent sort of American." They couldn't possibly have been any more *in*. England still had what the journalists called Smart Society—a blend of pedigree, money, and talent, the beau and haute monde combined—and Fred and Adele Astaire found themselves very much in the thick of it.

Fred acquired an English valet, began his habit of buying racehorses, shopped Savile Row, eventually acquired a small black Rolls-Royce, known as a baby Rolls. The Astaires could have served as characters in an Anthony Powell novel, though perhaps Adele's raucous candor would have made her a better fit in Evelyn Waugh's *Vile Bodies*. They were comfortable in England, and the English were comfortable with them, on and off the stage. The Prince of Wales claimed to have seen their show *Stop Flirting* no fewer than ten times, and Fred made a note of the elegant cut of the lapels on the prince's white waistcoat, which he had English tailors imitate for him. James Barrie and George Bernard Shaw were both quite gone on Adele, with Barrie suggesting that she consider playing Peter Pan.

In America Jock Whitney and Alfred Vanderbilt were part of their circle, or, more accurately, the Astaires were part of theirs; Tallulah Bankhead, Somerset Maugham, Noël Coward, and Gertrude Lawrence were also friends. They were the toast of two continents. Even Fred, with what Henry James called an imagination of disaster, the dubious talent of always being able to see the worst of things, had little about which to complain. They were leading the good life, the high life, a fine breeze stirring them gently on their way in the fast lane.

The Astaires didn't suffer greatly during the Depression, which in fact was good for show business, causing people to seek out escapism more ardently than ever. In America, Flo Ziegfeld paid them five thousand dollars a week to be in one of his shows. They scored in *The Band Wagon*, a Broadway hit that Fred would later redo, with major surgery, as a movie with Cyd Charisse. The reviews they received sounded as if they had written them themselves. Brooks Atkinson, the then still quite young *New York Times* theater critic, wrote, "This revue is without flaw." Other papers spoke of Fred's graduating from mere hoofer to a genuine comic talent. In the Astaire partnership, Fred was emerging from his role as the lesser, younger brother; some reviewers thought that he had surpassed his sister in energy and flair.

The last time Fred and Adele danced together on stage was March 5, 1932, in a road-company version of *The Band Wagon*. Nearly thirty-five, Adele was ready to toss in the taps, and did so by marrying the dipsomaniacal Charlie Cavendish. Adele was in most ways her brother's perfect partner; just the right size (5-foot-3 and 106 pounds), with great physical charm centering on her large eyes, wittily pouting mouth, and easy comic gifts. Their increased fame as a brother-and-sister act allowed them to ignore the need to dance romantically as a couple—"it's like kissing your sister" being an old saying suggesting an experience of the utterly thrill-free sort, unless of course one's taste runs to incest.

The only complaint Fred Astaire ever had against Adele was that she was not as hard a worker as he, not much given to the ardor for perfection that was central to his character. He was a man who lay awake at night working out ideas for new dances. She found rehearsals a drag, and perfection nice enough in its way, though scarcely worth giving up the charms of social life; certainly nothing to lie awake at night for, at least not alone.

With his sister's retirement, Fred Astaire faced the question of whether he could make it on his own. Before taking up that problem in earnest, he had met and fallen (perhaps the only serious fall in his adult career) in love with a divorcée named Phyllis Potter. She was roughly the same height as Adele, slender, and also, in looks, again like his sister, the type of the gamine. She was socially well connected, brought up by an aunt and uncle when her mother had remarried. The uncle, Henry Bull, was president of the Turf and Field Club; she pronounced her r's as w's, as in "Fweddie, Fweddie, dawling." According to Fred, when they first met, at a golf luncheon given by Mrs. Virginia Graham Fair Vanderbilt, Phyllis had never heard of him. He was thirty-two, she twenty-four, and he tactfully laid siege to her. His mother was less than pleased, thinking her son would make his way more easily in the world unencumbered by a divorced woman with a four-year-old son. Fred, not his mother, prevailed. He and his wife would have two children of their own, Fred, Jr., and Ava, neither of whom ever danced professionally.

Not much is known about Fred Astaire as a ladies' man. No stories exist about him as a masher, roué, or even a serious chaser. The man who taught America to dance "The Continental" ("You kiss while you're dancing"), who held Ginger Rogers, Rita Hayworth, Paulette Goddard, Audrey Hepburn, Barrie Chase, and other beautiful women in his arms, bending them gently backward, whirling them about—but who himself didn't often kiss on stage, claiming that he did his lovemaking with his feet—this same man seems to have been too well mannered and otherwise centered on his work to give women other than second place in his life. He was a faithful and good husband, whose life almost came apart when his wife died of lung cancer at the age of forty-six, leaving him a widower at fifty-four. He married again, in 1980 at the age of eighty, this time to a woman who was a former jockey named Robyn Smith. She was forty-three years younger than he and previously the squeeze of Alfred Vanderbilt, whose horses she sometimes rode. Robyn Smith, as the English say, saw Astaire out at his death at eighty-eight.

Lots of stories are told about Fred Astaire's entrée into Hollywood. The best known—alas, never authenticated —has to do with the unidentified studio operative who, after watching Astaire's screen test, is supposed to have reported: "Balding. Can't sing. Dances a little." In different versions the wording is altered slightly.

In fact, David O. Selznick, then the head of RKO, though soon to become an executive at MGM, where his father-in-law Louis B. Mayer most powerfully presided, thought Fred Astaire likely to be a great movie per-

former. "I am tremendously enthused about the suggestion New York [by which he meant his agents there] has
made of using Fred Astaire," he wrote in 1933 to two un-
derlings at RKO. "If he photographs (I have ordered a
test), he may prove to be a really sensational bet. . . . Astaire is one of the great artists of the day: a magnificent
performer, a man conceded to be perhaps, next to Leslie
Howard, the most charming in the American theater, and
unquestionably the outstanding young leader of American musical comedy." Selznick later showed some hesita-
tion, but didn't finally back down: "I am a little uncertain
about the man, but I feel, in spite of his enormous ears
and bad chin line, that his charm is so tremendous that it
comes through even in this wretched [screen] test, and I
would be perfectly willing to go ahead with him [in a
movie then in the planning stage]."

MGM signed Fred Astaire to a three-week contract at
fifteen hundred dollars per week. He was to dance, playing a character named Fred Astaire, with Joan Crawford
in an eminently forgettable flick called *Dancing Lady*.
They gave him, in other words, a shot. He volleyed it
back at them for an authoritative winner. Whatever his
screen test might have shown, whatever his physical
deficiencies, Fred Astaire came across splendidly on the
screen. He was the masculine equivalent of what the

French call a *belle laide:* a feature-by-feature homely woman who is somehow nevertheless stunning. His attractiveness may have resided partly in his clothes and the way he wore them; it had a great deal to do, of course, with the way he moved, including his most casual moves. Whatever the magical ingredients that made for movie charm, he possessed them. He lit up the joint—any joint he may have been in—turning the silver screen quite golden.

Of what did Astaire's magic consist? Why even now, more than twenty years after his death, more than fifty years since the days of his prime as a dancer-singer-actor, why do his old movies still shimmer with glamour, why do so many people still find the sight and sound of him enchanting, why does the very idea of Fred Astaire continue to cast its own lovely lilting glow? We are, my dear Watson, obviously in the presence of a mystery.

Peculiar Looking

This mystery is heightened in the case of Fred Astaire, who may be said to have done extraordinarily well what may not have been all that much worth doing in the first place—at least not until he came along and did it with a hitherto unimagined brio. But what, really, did he do? He frisked about in tap shoes, he twirled beautiful women around waxen floors, he sang in a less than commanding voice songs other people wrote. From this, as the old Jews used to say, he made a living? He did indeed, and a very impressive one; and he also cut out a permanent place for himself in the history of entertainment, quite probably in that of art. But how, more precisely, was this possible?

Through practice, practice, practice, one less than satisfying answer is. Through great natural style, also known as towering talent, another answer has it. Through the luck of the time in which he performed his minor but charming arts—a time, the Depression days of the 1930s, when frivolity and irrelevant elegance seemed uplifting, even, some claim, psychologically restorative. Yet these and other explanations don't quite explain Fred Astaire's magic either. Magic, perhaps we ought to remember, is magic, prima facie, because it cannot be altogether successfully explained. Once entirely explained, of course, the magic, *poof!*, is gone.

Let us begin by considering the first thing Fred Astaire, that most attractive of men, had to overcome, which was his less than impressive physical appearance. "Seeing themselves on the screen is usually a chore for most performers," Astaire wrote in *Steps in Time*, his rather matter-of-fact account of his career. "In my case, it's frightening because I've always thought myself rather peculiar." *Peculiar* is not an imprecise word to describe his looks, with no *rather* about it.

Starting at the top, Astaire's head was too large, quite out of proportion with his small and slender body and narrow shoulders. Long, too, it was, way too long, cursedly, horse-facedly long. Atop this oddly proportioned, ill-shaped skull, the hair early receded, began to fall out, was depressingly sparse in its residue. By the time he went to Hollywood to dance and otherwise cavort before the remorseless close-ups of movie cameras, Fred Astaire required what in his autobiography he referred to as "hair embellishments," more commonly and variously known as toupees, toops, rugs, pieces.

Meticulous—a word whose exact meaning is more than merely careful but edging over into fussiness— meticulous in all aspects of his appearance, Astaire searched lifelong for the perfect hairpiece, which he felt eluded him no less completely than the perfect society eluded Vladimir Ilyich Lenin. In *Bring on the Empty Horses*, one of his memoirs of his Hollywood days, David Niven, a neighbor and friend of the Astaires, tells that Fred, to "maintain the status quo" of saving what hair he had, acquired "an electric hair restorer, a strange throbbing rubber cup containing elaborate coils and impulses. He must have misread the directions and assembled it incorrectly because on opening night it went into reverse and yanked out a large portion of what [hair] he had left."

Humphrey Bogart, Bing Crosby, Ray Milland, John Wayne, Frank Sinatra, Jimmy Stewart, among other famous male movie stars, wore hairpieces. In those days there were more rugs on Hollywood leading men than one might find in an extended Armenian family. Sinatra hired a woman whose sole job it was to look after his collection of twenty-six different pieces, which she carried around stored in attaché cases for a salary much greater than that of a high school teacher.

Not that Fred Astaire's various pieces were ridiculous; they weren't: they had a sheen, were parted on the left, leaving lots of skin showing at the temples. In later life, his hairpieces, which he wore without the sheen—something called "the dry look" had emerged—did seem obviously false, and a touch silly, and therefore a little sad. He would probably have done better to go au naturel, which is to say bald. Actually, he wore his pieces only on stage or in public performance. Like all men of his generation, he never went out of doors without a hat. When he danced—which means leapt, whirled, shwooshed, machine-gun fired his tapped shoes against floors, drums, furniture, walls—not a hair moved, but then neither, if memory serves, did Cary Grant's real hair move while he was climbing Mount Rushmore in *North by Northwest*.

The artificial, shiny slicked-down hair gave Astaire a slightly comic-book look, a bit like the villainous character Reggie in the old *Archie* comics. With his craving for perfection, how Astaire must have loathed having had to perform with his hairpiece on deck. Few photographs of him are available without his piece. One shows him at a nightclub, a wispiness atop his skull; the other, taken on the day of his marriage at City Hall in New York, demonstrates that the absence of hair further elongates his already too long face.

A reviewer who once commented on Astaire's hairpiece got a letter from the dancer stating that he had gone too far. When the cameras went off at the end of *Blue Skies*, which he thought would be his last movie, Astaire is said to have ripped off his piece, stomped on it with great unambiguous glee, as if to say at least I won't have to wear this son-of-a-bitching thing any more. But he went on to do more movies.

He had a wide forehead, wide and high, a touch Neanderthalish in the way, if we look closely, it hung slightly over his eyes. This took some attention away from those eyes, which were hooded and blue, made to look very blue in the Technicolor films he did, but not otherwise notable for depth or penetration. In some of his movies, he looks as if he might have what is called a "lazy eye" (his left one), which opened less fully than his right eye, especially when he sang. He is said to have had a mole under this same left eye that, for movies, was covered over by makeup. Maybe his looks would have been improved if this defect had been allowed to show, but he performed in the era of the touch-up artist, when flaws were verboten. Maybe the touching up was for the best: there was about Fred Astaire's looks, there was meant to be about them, something highly polished that precluded the kind of reality implicit in the appearance of a mole. "The arrangement of your features," Cyd Charisse, playing the Soviet commissar Ninotchka in *Silk Stockings*, says to him, "is not entirely repulsive to me." Nor was it to most women.

David O. Selznick referred to Astaire's ears as "enormous." They were large and fleshy, and they stuck out, though not appallingly so. From some angles they could seem pointy at the tips. But the big ears that were Clark Gable's also stuck out, in Gable's case emphatically so, and certainly didn't stop him from being one of the great Hollywood romantic leading men of his day. Bing Crosby had huge ears, and even the dashing Cary Grant's ears stuck out. As a big-eared man myself, stick-out division, I am a close student of these appendages, and my authoritative opinion is that Astaire would have looked rather more freakish with small ears that clung to his skull. Astaire's ears came to seem more prominent as he grew older, just as his wigs came to seem less convincing, but then he was no longer under pressure of coming on as a figure of glamour, and it much less mattered.

Astaire's nose was straight, largish, perhaps too fleshy at the tip, which has a slight dent, giving it, viewed straight on, an asymmetrical look. From some camera angles it seems to dominate his face in a less than winning way. His mouth was wide, upper lip very thin under an emphatic philtrum, that vertical line that runs downward from nose to upper lip, but it could command a dazzling smile, witty and warm. When the smile works, which it almost always does, it makes us forget about Astaire's chin, which, as Selznick noted, has a bad line. Not so much strong as long, his chin allowed caricaturists, Al Hirschfeld among them, to draw him in profile with chin and nose threatening to meet, looking rather like a witch in a top hat. Directors arranged for this profile view of his chin to be hidden as well as possible from most camera angles.

In profile, sitting at the piano with a cigarette in his mouth, as he did in a scene from *Follow the Fleet*, Fred Astaire looks a bit like Hoagy Carmichael. The thinness of his face, its angularity and gauntness, sometimes makes him resemble a jockey, one of those hard-bitten bony little guys who've ridden more than a thousand nags. (In England, jockeys were among his friends.) Wearing a derby, as he did in a scene in *Top Hat* and in a few other movies, with his long face and large ears and extended chin, he looks like nothing so much as a double for Stan Laurel. A sweet goofy look, to be sure, but scarcely the preferred look for a leading man. In most of the movie stills of Astaire, at least those in which he is not dancing, he looks—how to say it?—not all that intelligent. His is a face most interesting in animation, and most interesting of all when enraptured in his arts of singing and dancing.

He was slender to the point of, but just evading, skinniness. In *Follow the Fleet* he appears in a scene in a T-shirt. A mistake. Such scenes are generally meant to be somewhat provocative in a sexual way; recall Marlon Brando's wife-beater undershirts in *A Streetcar Named Desire*. When still young, Paul Newman on screen was always walking around in boxer shorts. Wife-beaters worked for Brando, boxers for Newman; T-shirts didn't for Astaire.

A T-shirt revealed how thin he was, how narrow were his shoulders, which tended to slope a bit when he wasn't dancing. His arms show some sinew—he must have been reasonably strong to be able to lift and toss his various dance partners around, though such lifting and tossing was not a regular feature of his suave moves on the dance floor—but little muscularity. He looks a bit like the ninety-eight-pound weakling who gets sand kicked in his face in the old Charles Atlas muscle-building ads that ran on the backs of comic books in the 1940s.

Astaire's shoe size was a normal 8½. But his hands were disproportionately large. They seemed the hands of a farm worker, real meat hooks. The thumbs are too long, the fingers flat across the top. He attempted to make them appear smaller when on camera by curling up his middle fingers. The reason the largeness of his hands is noticeable is that Fred Astaire was what is known as a full-body dancer. As he danced, all parts of his body were carefully deployed; after his feet, his hands most prominently so, hands that he sometimes appeared to want to hide. In some photo stills, we note one of these hands, fingers curled under, on the waist of Ginger Rogers or Rita Hayworth. "My hands are huge," he told Leslie Caron. "Look at them. In ballet you've got to hold your hands so gracefully, and my hands are so big that I would look ridiculous [doing so]." Miss Caron adds that "he always held his third and fourth fingers almost on top of each other to minimize the size of his hands."

A famous perfectionist, he rehearsed even his hands. The television producer Bob Mackie, with whom Astaire did one of his television specials, recalls that he "wouldn't just rehearse the words [of songs], he would rehearse how his hand went into his pocket and how he would stand with just his thumb out, and how he would hold his hands in a certain way."

Long-waisted, Astaire hadn't much torso. Wearing his pants high, in the style of the era, added to his look of being all legs; his femurs, those bones above the knee extending to the hip, appeared especially lengthy. Unlike such wide-bottomed romantic leads as Gable, Grant, and Robert Mitchum, he had no discernible rear end.

If it is godly to be thin, as in our age it has been deemed to be, then Astaire was among the gods, or at a minimum among the favorites of the gods for not having to do anything to maintain his thinness. Insofar as is known, he never dieted. "What is a calorie, anyway?" he asked Benny Green, the English jazz critic who wrote an appropriately slender book about him. He weighed roughly 130 pounds. He obviously danced off all he ate, but even in later life, retired as a dancer, he never showed the least sign of a paunch, love handles, or any of the other fleshly accoutrements that stalk most men as they slide into middle age and beyond. His was the perfect body for dinner clothes. Comparing his own body with that of Fred Astaire, Gene Kelly once said that in a tuxedo, Astaire's natural costume, he, Kelly, looked like a truck driver out on a date.

How tall was Fred Astaire? Here we enter the realm of insignificant controversy. His height has been variously given as between 5-foot-7 and 5-10. As a man of 5-7 myself—if I stand up straight—I naturally favor the shorter Astaire, and have given the matter careful scrutiny. (Lots of smallish leading men in the Hollywood of those days: John Garfield, James Cagney, Humphrey Bogart, George Raft, Spencer Tracy, Edward G. Robinson, and others.) Astaire's thinness, his long legs, the kind of clothes he wore and the way he wore them (short jackets, high trousers), all contributed to make him seem taller than he was. Finding dance partners smaller than he was always a concern.

Astaire fails the comparative height test. In most scenes in which other men appear, he is usually the smallest man in the scene. In the early movies he made with Randolph Scott—*Roberta, Follow the Fleet*—he seems positively diminutive. Tallish women—Cyd Charisse, Eleanor Powell—had to wear flats when dancing with him. My guess is that the studios, in choosing male choruses to dance behind him, put a height restriction on most of the dancers: no one over 5-foot-10, tops, allowed. Like too tall a diver or gymnast, too tall a dancer probably isn't a good idea. The dancer Tommy Tune, at more than 6-foot-6, has always seemed like Samuel Johnson's dog dancing on his hind legs: the wonder is that he can do it at all. Good actors and great dancers can make themselves seem taller than they actually are. Here Astaire qualified: he was a short man who arranged never to allow himself to appear short.

The general effect of Fred Astaire physically was of someone so polished that he sometimes seemed slightly cartoonish. "Mr. Astaire," Graham Greene wrote in a misbegotten review of *Top Hat*, "is the nearest approach we are ever likely to have to a human Mickey Mouse; he might have been drawn by Mr. Walt Disney, with his quick physical wit, his incredible agility." I myself think Fred Astaire looked more like Max Beerbohm's drawings of himself as a young man. Sleek is the word that best defines the Astaire look for me, sleek, kempt, elegant.

Feature by feature, part by part, Fred Astaire was neither rugged nor effeminate. He was—no other word for it—Astairish. "I was a weird-looking character anyway and I never liked the way I photographed," he once said about himself. "And I don't think the studios did either, when they tested me in the beginning. But they got so used to it that it didn't matter. So long as you had some sort of personality that worked. That's what counted. You didn't have to be a handsome dog any more." True enough, through the 1930s and '40s and even into the '50s, leading men in the movies didn't have to be beautiful, or even good-looking: Cagney, Bogart, Robinson, and William and Dick Powell are notable examples.

What was needed was to leave the impress of a distinct—and distinctly interesting—persona. Here Fred Astaire, clearly, qualified.

James Agate, the English theater critic, reviewing the stage production of *Gay Divorce*, claimed that "Mr. Astaire's secret is that of the late Rudolph Valentino and of Mr. Maurice Chevalier—sex, but sex so bejeweled and be-glamoured and be-pixied that the weaker vessels who fall for it can pretend that it isn't sex at all but a sublimated Barriesque projection of the Little Fellow with the Knuckles in his eyes. You'd have thought by the look of the first night foyer that it was Mothering Thursday, since every woman in the place was urgent to take to her bosom this waif with the sad eyes and the twinkling feet. Ah, yes, to pretend that it wasn't sex at all." I wonder. My sense is that sex isn't what Fred Astaire was primarily about. Something else, something quite different, was going on.

"Was he good-looking?" asked Audrey Hepburn, who danced with Fred Astaire in the movie *Funny Face*, and then answered her own question: "I think so, because charm is the best-looking thing in the world, isn't it?"

Man Makes the Clothes

Despite the little catalogue I've just compiled of the oddities of Fred Astaire's physique, his charm was preponderantly physical, deriving from the way he moved, especially, of course, the way he moved on the dance floor, though not there exclusively. The dancer and choreographer Bob Fosse claimed that he could spot Astaire from a distance by the rhythm of his walk. The way he talked, his gestures, and not least his clothes and the way he wore them were also distinctive. Clothes make the man, an old haberdasher's slogan had it, and they went a long way toward making Astaire, though in his case the man also helped make the clothes. Much of his charm was in his style, and his clothes contributed a vast deal to the Astaire style.

Fred Astaire always dressed thoughtfully. The earliest photographs of him show a well-turned-out young man. He had instinctive good taste. Hanging out with the Ivy League boys who pursued his sister must have given him a few further pointers about wearing clothes well: Brooks Brothers, J. Press sorts of pointers.

On his first trip to England, Fred Astaire turned from a young man who was well groomed and carefully dressed into someone close to what used to be called a fashion plate. He became mid-Atlantic in his taste in clothes; his speech, with its splendidly clear diction, seemed a touch mid-Atlantic, too. He found himself admiring the clothes of the British aristocracy. Obtaining the correct shirt studs became for him a serious matter. In the movie *Swing Time*, there is even a little sartorial joke, in which his character convinces his rival for the affections of Penny (Ginger Rogers), the Latin American bandleader called Ricardo (played by Georges Metaxa), that he has to send out his wedding trousers to a tailor because they don't have cuffs, then arranges that he gets trousers returned to him that are impossibly large, too large, certainly, for him to walk up the aisle, let alone hope to marry Penny in.

Astaire looked great in tails (which he claimed to take no pleasure in wearing), in a tuxedo, in suits (single- or double-breasted), in blazers, in sport jackets and trousers. But think of all the outfits it is nearly impossible to imagine him wearing: visualize him in a football uniform, a Nehru jacket, a tank top, Spandex shorts, a Speedo, a baseball cap turned backward, a backpack, a ponytail, jeans stonewashed, relaxed fit, or any other kind. Not possible! He wore an enlisted man's navy uniform in *Follow the Fleet*, and only the trousers, emphasizing his long legs, seemed to work. Everything else made him look skinny, bony, dopey even. Nor is it easy to imagine him in disarray: unshaven, rumpled, scruffy, or scuffy-shoed.

Today it is difficult to see anyone else in white tie and tails, especially on a dance floor, without thinking of Fred Astaire. He was the first man to sing the swell Irving Berlin song "Top Hat, White Tie, and Tails," which was written for him and which he made his own, and the getup soon enough became his trademark. Astaire was a dandy, defined by Carlyle as a clothes-wearing man. Good clothes, careful dress, a certain look was expected of him, and he almost never disappointed.

"It is only the shallow people," said Oscar Wilde, "who do not judge by appearance." Fred Astaire would have understood.

The director Billy Wilder reported having a dream, many times repeated, in which he is asking Fred Astaire where he buys his clothes, and just when Astaire is about to tell him, Wilder wakes up. (Astaire's chief source for suits was the London tailoring firm of Anderson and Sheppard.) Even had Astaire vouchsafed him the answer, I fear that it wouldn't have done poor Wilder, a witty but squat and pudgy man, much good. One had to be shaped like Fred Astaire—light, lithe, long-legged—to bring off his look of casual elegance. Apart from his white-tie and tails getup, Astaire wore clothes in a happily tossed off way. He knew clothes could be amusing, witty even, but also that it wouldn't do to seem to make too much of them, to convey that too much thought went into their selection. Elegance, even slightly overdone, ends in foppishness.

Fairly early in life, Astaire learned that the best clothes are the clothes in which one looks and feels most comfortable. He understood that one doesn't ever want one's clothes to look too new; a little worn, lived in, was always to be preferred. One thinks here of Johnny Carson, slender, taller than Astaire, who never looked comfortable in his clothes—clothes so stiff-seeming that they made him look as if he had neglected to remove the hangers from his suit and sport jackets.

Hats reduced the lengthiness of Fred Astaire's face. Top hats and fedoras he brought off supremely, both in the spirit of casualness. He wore top hats at exactly the right angle. He was one of the few men who could wear a porkpie hat and not seem a perfect doofus. Derbies, as I said earlier, didn't for him do. My guess is that he wouldn't have looked too great in a yachting cap, either. A Homburg was too earnest, too formal, too much the banker or diplomat. In a straw boater he was a knockout, the American Maurice Chevalier, maybe a bit better.

The only man in Hollywood who wore better neckties than Astaire was Cary Grant, though Astaire, a smaller man, could bring off bowties, wearing them in a way that suggested good-humored jauntiness, while Grant was too large and full-chested to do so, except in a tuxedo. His pocket squares, worn in the left-side suit pocket, felt exactly right, a fine finishing touch. On him a boutonniere looked not excessive but dashing. Alone among American actors, he wore ascots without seeming pretentious. His shirts, doubtless custom-made, were perfect, just the right softness, just the right colors: he wears a swell yellow button-down-collar shirt while playing drums in an early scene in *Daddy Long Legs;* a perfect pink shirt with matching socks in *Silk Stockings,* a gray-blue double-breasted suit with a well-worn brown fedora keeping things from looking too studied. I don't recall ever seeing him in anything monogrammed. "What's the matter," I once heard a man say to another man who had monograms on the cuffs of his shirts, "having trouble remembering your own name?"

When Astaire wore sport jackets, they seemed pliant, richly textured, and buttery soft. In *The Band Wagon* he travels in a wonderfully muted rust brown subdued tweed jacket. His trousers with their outward pleats, a slight break at the ankle, worn high on the waist, hang just right. As with his white tie and tails, so with his more casual clothes, everything needed to be ready to be danced in on sudden notice.

Because one's eyes were so much on his feet, the shoes Fred Astaire wore were important. None of them was outré. Apart from black patent leather for his white-tie and tails getups, he tended to wear sporty shoes: brown suedes, the occasional pair of saddle shoes, and (in *Flying Down to Rio*) white bucks worn with horizontally striped socks, two-color co-respondent shoes (so-named, I have been told by a worldly wise lawyer, himself a dab dresser, because they are often the shoe of choice worn by men named as co-respondents in divorce cases). Somehow all of Astaire's shoes on their soles mysteriously bore taps.

Astaire was also good at throwing together what might normally seem discordant colors but which on him worked well. Brown suede loafers, say, with a taupe blue double-breasted suit. Or a buff-colored, slightly beaten-up fedora with a tuxedo. A French semiologist could doubtless do a lengthy and jargon-laden study of the colors of his socks. The point is that he made the normally discordant seem not in the least discordant but instead interesting, striking. Elegant is as elegant does.

Lots of people think Astaire's sometimes wearing a necktie in place of a belt a fine flamboyant touch, but I am not among them. I thought it went over the line of flair and into the land of fey. He didn't do badly, though, with colorful silk bandanas tied loosely around his throat. In later life, he understood that a bit of color at the throat, along with covering over the sagging skin at the neck, enlivens an older face. His pocket squares were never too showy. He looked good in bathrobes, too, though on him they were elevated to dressing gowns.

Because of his clothes, but because of his grooming and his dancing, too, Fred Astaire qualifies as a member in excellent standing in the long line of dandies, beginning in Regency England with Beau Brummell. The line of the modern dandy extends from Brummell to Benjamin Disraeli to Robert de Montesquiou to Max Beerbohm to Fred Astaire to, in the current day, Tom Wolfe. The dandy specializes in superb taste done in a simple mode (Disraeli, who tended to overdress, was always pushing it, as does, perhaps, Mr. Wolfe). But the dandy is everywhere a man cool and detached, who always looks good without appearing to have gone to much strain to do so.

Astaire, at least in his movie roles, was always the dandy. But he was a dandy with a difference. He somehow managed to look effortlessly, elegantly, but not necessarily expensively well dressed—he was the very model, in this regard, of the democratic dandy, itself an innovative figure.

He took care, wrote Henry James of the coldly elegant Gilbert Osmond, in *The Portrait of a Lady*, "to have no vulgar things." In a few of his movies, Astaire wore an identification bracelet on the same wrist as his watch; a minor mistake—a small vulgar thing—but in a man so perfectly turned out any excess seems a wretched one. The only garment Astaire ever wore in the movies that seems really quite hopeless is the white raincoat in which he dances, toward the close of *Funny Face*, with Audrey Hepburn. That coat is too white; it's not even a particularly good fit, but appears a size or two too large. The coat appears to be wearing him. At times it looks as if Audrey Hepburn is dancing not with the world's greatest dancer but with a white raincoat with some little guy inside. He also wears a damn sad striped blazer in *The Story of Vernon and Irene Castle*, which is also ill-fitting. Mistakes happen; if they didn't, how would we gauge perfection?

Astaire could make double-breasted suits look casual, single-breasted ones (lounge suits, even heavily patterned racetrack suits) seem natural. Sport jackets, double-vented, he wore with aplomb. His suits and jackets of natural shoulders were cut high under the armpits, made of soft fabrics, cut roomy (to dance in), suave yet sensible. With only a few exceptions—a belted sport jacket he wore in *Roberta* comes to mind—many of the clothes he wore in the movies of the 1930s and '40s could be worn today without seeming at all dated. And why shouldn't they, since Ralph Lauren and other designers have sedulously copied them, no doubt with Fred Astaire at least partially in mind, and continue selling clothes that look like them in our day?

In its summer 2007 catalogue, the J. Peterman Company advertises a wristwatch under the rubric "Memories of Mr. Astaire." The copy runs: "Fred Astaire made it OK to be on the sophisticated side. He didn't have an English accent. He wasn't stuck up. He was like a regular person, except that he had talent and could sweep women off their feet. He knew all about the best things in life, too. He ordered his suits on Savile Row. Before he wore them, he'd throw them against the wall a few times. 'Get that stiff squareness out,' he said. You could learn a lot from Mr. Astaire. This watch brings him back for me.

The mellow, debonair look he favored when he wasn't in top hat and tails, combined with a super-duper self-winding movement introduced in the 1930s." (The watch being advertised, incidentally, isn't all that elegant, costs $498, and doesn't in the least suggest Fred Astaire, but let that pass.)

"The democratic ideal: a classless aristocrat" is what G. Bruce Boyer, in *Fred Astaire Style,* a small book about Astaire's clothes, calls Fred Astaire in his movie roles. The aristocracy in question is of course that of talent, which in a democracy trumps that of birth and even that of money. "Time and time again in the Astaire-Rogers films," Boyer writes, "nonchalance defeats formality, heritage succumbs to natural finesse, vitality overcomes rigid ceremony, propriety is bested by humor, ritual dignity by legitimate naiveté." The aristocracy of talent is of course the best of all aristocracies, and the one to which to belong. Fred Astaire found exactly the right clothes, comfortably worn, befitting this small but swell class that he more than anyone else helped create.

A Litvak Passes Through

A group of songs and more or less energetic dances strung out over a generally preposterous plot, such is musical comedy, a purely American art form. Along with jazz, it is one of the few original American contributions to the world's stock of entertainments. From the 1920s through the 1950s, it flourished, owing to a small number of talented and prolific songwriters, some of whose names, it may well be, will live longer than those of the country's greatest poets: Irving Berlin, Cole Porter, Jerome Kern, Richard Rodgers, Lorenz Hart, Oscar Hammerstein, the brothers Gershwin, and a small number of others. Talent of the kind that went into these Broadway musicals, and into musical movies, flashed across the sky and, *whoosh!*, was never to show up again.

Samuel Taylor Coleridge, the Romantic poet and critic, coined the immensely helpful phrase "willing suspension of disbelief." Although not a phrase one can dance to, it has its uses: applied to the reading or viewing of works of art, it means that, to appreciate many of them, one must close off one's normal skepticism, common sense, even sense of reality. Watching *Oedipus Rex*, for example, it won't do to ask how a young man can be so stupid as to marry a woman much older than he without bothering to ask where she came from or whether she had been married before or—might it just be?—had any children. Ask these questions and the play never gets out of New Haven. Probability must not be consulted; disbelief must be suspended.

With musical comedies, disbelief must not be merely suspended but hanged by the neck until dead. (The situation is not much better in opera, where vastly overweight men and women, when stabbed, or as like as not having stabbed themselves, react by immediately beginning to sing loudly.) Many people are easily able to make this suspension of disbelief; some make it gladly. I have seen men with strong Mafia connections much moved by *The Pajama Game* or *My Fair Lady*; female divorce lawyers, scrap-iron dealers, ruthless borax men brought near tears by *A Chorus Line* and beyond tears by *Fiddler on the Roof.*

Putting musical comedies on film first resulted in spectaculars: above all, the geometrical-minded Busby Berkeley bringing his dancers out of fountains, down from clouds, peeping out of immense pools, with feathers, fans, boots, headdresses flapping and flying all over the joint. The effect was cheerleading to the highest power, marching bands without the instruments, the result less entertaining than amazing. Two questions, though, arise: Who would want to do this? And why am I watching it?

Soon enough it became understood that the real advantage of film, for musicals, contra Busby Berkeley, was the close-up. Close-ups permitted facial expressions. The close-up allowed men and women to sing into each other's faces at a distance of six inches or less. Being sung to, loudly, at such close proximity by a man whose first name is Nelson or Ezio would not, let us agree, be everyone's idea of a corking good time, but during a certain period it was thought highly romantic. The suspension of disbelief button here had to be pressed with real force.

But the close-up camera also allowed one to focus on two dancers, or one dancer, or the dancer's feet doing astonishing things. Fred Astaire came to be a genius at knowing how the camera caught each part of his body.

Nor while he was dancing did he permit the camera to cut away to focus on his feet or switch to his face; he made sure it took in all his body.

As for the plots of movie musicals, they call for a willing suspension not merely of disbelief but of rationality. James Agate remarked of the Astaire-Rogers movies that "apart from the dancing of these two artists, they are deserts of witlessness." He saw their movie *Roberta* on a wet night in Blackpool, and vowed that "rather than drown in another dose of such inanity I would climb the Eiffel Tower hand over fist and commit suicide in someone's backyard. I will go farther and say that not for twenty minutes of Irving [not Berlin but Sir Henry] or Sarah Bernhardt would I again endure such drivel." This is strong but not entirely crazy.

Consider *Roberta*, the movie that drove Agate so bonkers. RKO made it just as Astaire and Rogers's *Gay Divorcee* was resoundingly clanging the gong of commercial success. So many of these movies pivot on mistaken identities, goofy misalliances, even malapropisms. *Roberta* begins on the latter: a heavily accented, half-crazed white Russian who runs a nightclub in Paris hires Huck Haines (Astaire) and his band, the Wabash Indianians, under the impression that they are actually American Indians. When he finds out that they aren't Indians but Indianians, simple Hoosiers, he wants nothing to do with them. John Kent (Randolph Scott), a football All-American, who happens to be traveling with the band, also just happens to have an aunt in Paris who has become a famous couturier, running an exclusive shop called Roberta's. On the staff at Roberta's is the Countess Tanka Scharwenka, who is in fact Lizzie Gatz, a former neighbor and girlfriend of Astaire's back in Indiana. (Yo, you still there?) Lots of white Russians, snobbish Americans, balalaika music, comic drunks appear. (As S. J. Perelman, in his parodies of screenplays, used to note, "A Litvak passes through.") I could continue with this plot summary, but why insult both of us? Suffice to say that it all ends in a fashion show with Fred Astaire singing "Lovely to Look At," and Fred and Ginger dancing for the second time to "I Won't Dance." Randolph Scott goes off with a white Russian princess (played by Irene Dunne), Astaire with Rogers. The larger point is that the theater of the absurd started well before the advent of Samuel Beckett, Eugene Ionesco, Harold Pinter, and the rest of the dark playwrights—absurdity to the highest power really began in the musical comedy movies of the 1930s and '40s.

Of course the plot in most movie musicals is only the excuse to set up the songs and dances and comic bits. "What do you expect from a musical anyway?" asked the movie and jazz critic Otis Ferguson, who, answering his own question, replied: "A musical rarely attempts to be more than a ragbag of various show tricks; and even when it does, there is no relation between its comedy, which is mostly wisecracks, and its songs, which are mostly sugar."

Ferguson goes on to maintain that there are essentially two plots in movie musicals: "the Hymie-the-Hoofer type, where the boy makes the grade with his act; the My-Gal-Daisy-She-Durrives-Me-Crazy type, where the boy makes the girl." A variation on these is that the girl finds some reason utterly to loathe the boy, causing the boy of course to bring her all the way round to falling helplessly in love with him. (A big song-and-dance number, if you happen to have one on you, usually does this particular trick.) The rest has to do with the not very arduous task of finding a way, in the first number, to elide from regular conversation into song, preferably accompanied by a highly energetic tap dance.

In most of his movies, Astaire plays a variation on Hymie-the-Hoofer. Sometimes he is also a band leader or a trumpeter (as in *Second Chorus*), or a hoofer in the navy (as in *Follow the Fleet*), or a con man (*Yolanda and the Thief*), or a con man–hoofer (*Shall We Dance*), or a gambler (*Swing Time*), or a multimillionaire businessman who just happens to keep a full set of drums in his office for a big drumming-while-dancing number (in *Daddy Long Legs*), or (most frequently) a professional dancer (*Top Hat, You Were Never Lovelier, You'll Never Get Rich*, and others), an air force ace (*The Sky's the Limit*), or sometimes a retired hoofer making a comeback (as in *The Band Wagon*); in *Carefree* he is a shrink, and in *Funny Face* a professional photographer. The plots of these movies run into one another, so that, even for someone who has thought a fair amount about them, it isn't easy to keep straight which is which. But, mirabile dictu, whatever his profession, Astaire always seems to go to work in shoes with taps on them and somewhere in the background a twenty-five-piece orchestra hovers at the ready.

Like Maurice Chevalier before him, Astaire in his movie roles is essentially the type of the boulevardier, a man who, whatever his ostensible work, is not, let us say, tied down by it. He is fundamentally unserious, without a lot on his mind except dressing nattily, dancing dazzlingly, and winning the girl handily, which inevitably he does. But in his movie roles Astaire could be a dentist or certified public accountant or funeral director or even on crutches, and the boys in Hollywood would have found a way to get him onto the dance floor, where he would proceed to win the girl and blow everyone in the audience away.

The overriding point of the absurd scripts of all these movies is that, in the end, talent will tell, and charm disarm—and, with Astaire in command, both do exactly that, just about every time.

Charmed, I'm Sure

Gifts come from God, presents from men and women. Serious talent is largely a gift from God. Charm is a present men and women bestow upon one another. No one is born charming, though charm comes fairly easily to some and is apparently quite impossible for others.

Charm has to do with pleasing, light-handedly, sometimes to the point of fascination. He or she "turned on the charm," we say, by which we mean that a man or woman cast a spell, however fleeting. Temporary enchantment is the state to which a charming person brings us. Charm is a performance of a kind; it is virtuosity of the personality. Charm is confident, never strained, always at ease in the world. Charm is not pushing; it has a fine sense of proportion and measure, never goes too far, never stays too long. Charm is Noël Coward, entering a party wearing an ordinary suit, discovering every other man in the room dressed in white tie and tails, and blithely announcing, "Please, I don't want anyone to apologize for overdressing."

Charm is elegance made casual, with emphasis on the casual. Charm mustn't seem too studied, forced, overdone. So many of the letters of Marcel Proust, during his youthful days of sucking up to the aristocracy, provide examples of charm overdone. They are heavy-handed, go on too much. Here is Proust writing to Robert de Montesquiou, in the summer of 1894 (Proust is twenty-three at the time): "I have no need to tell you that you were spoken of constantly with affectionate veneration and that your memory is much to be thanked for so graciously and nobly accompanying or rather guiding us on this excursion, which it diverted and embellished." I don't think so; I don't think anyone, least of all the sly and malevolent Montesquiou, likely for even a moment to have bought it. Charm is never so creamy, so smarmy; putting it on a bit thick is what our little Marcel is guilty of here and in a number of other letters to those he took to be his social betters. He would later learn otherwise, and became charming only when he acted in true character: the character, that is, of the penetratingly brilliant social analyst who discovered that the upper classes can be quite as swinish as the lower, in some ways even more so.

As Fred Astaire knew in his light bones, charm is bright, breezy, pleasing in and of itself. Charm knows when to turn itself off, when to depart, which is why it is invariably wanted back. Charm puts things interestingly, amusingly, surprisingly, sometimes originally, but never heavily, never too insistently; charm is the young Truman Capote, not the older Richard Wagner. Charm avoids cliché; it is ever fresh. Uncharming, if not untrue, is to say that D. H. Lawrence was a writer with many pernicious and ugly ideas. Charm (speaking here through Max Beerbohm) says, "Poor D. H. Lawrence. He never realized, don't you know—he never suspected that to be stark, staring mad is somewhat of a handicap for a writer."

So many traditions of charm are European or Asian in their provenance. English charm, French charm, Italian charm are perhaps the chief variants. One doesn't, somehow, think of Germans as charming, though perhaps Marlene Dietrich and Oskar Werner came close to putting this stereotype out to pasture. The Chinese and Japanese are of course not without their own elegant, if perhaps more formulaic, traditions of charm.

Cary Grant, who despite his immitigably English accent often played Americans, was English charm at its bounciest and least effete; Ronald Colman was English charm at its most suave. Charles Boyer was French charm in its romantic vein; Maurice Chevalier in its frivolous, frothy one. Marcello Mastroianni was a marvelous exemplar of Italian charm, and he could do charm in a thousand guises: elegant, comic, seedy, world-weary, and just about any other that was required. Russian charm is George Balanchine, a great artist who could do light and heavy charm, with an equally authoritative touch, and who could seem intimate while remaining coolly impersonal. Vladimir Nabokov worked much the same charm.

Americans can be amusing, hilarious, winning, immensely attractive, yet seldom full-out charming. Bing Crosby could exhibit a limited charm in the casual manner; Sinatra could do tough-guy charm, though I, for one, stopped being susceptible to it by the time I was thirty and preferred that he just shut up and keep singing. Charm tends to the aristocratic, and American charm, in the nature of the case, doesn't quite qualify. When it attempts an aristocratic tinge, it comes off as fake English or stuffily European. American charm, to be truly American, has somehow to combine the aristocratic with the democratic, while straining out all traces of snobbery.

American charm, at least as on exhibit in the movies, was best portrayed by Fred Astaire. Although he dressed

English-aristocratic, in his movies Astaire always bore boy-next-door American names such as Pete Peters or Huck Haines. In most of Astaire's movies, his manner was sometimes just slightly big city wise-guy, but also gee-whiz small town.

Contrast Fred Astaire with William Powell, whose suavity helped make the *Thin Man* movies so delightful. Powell in his movie persona is sophisticated in a way Astaire in his movie persona is distinctly not. Powell's character is world-weary, properly cynical, looking forward only to another of his perfectly confected cocktails. Astaire breaks out the champagne from time to time, and in one of his movies (*The Sky's the Limit*) he actually gets drunk, but his drunkenness turns out to be no more than an excuse to do a dance atop the bar. Like Astaire, Powell is always handsomely tailored, lives in starkly white plush apartments, drives flashy cars. But the good life, one might say, is all that is left to him, since he has previously seen the rest of life for what it really is. Powell's lack of enthusiasm, his witty cynicism, are among the chief marks of his sophistication; Astaire, urbane yet not entirely sophisticated, retains his enthusiasm, for the girl, for the song, above all for the dance. You can't dance the way Astaire did and come across as cynical, too—it wouldn't work.

And yet, regular guy though he is supposed to be in his movie roles, there is also always something more than a touch aristocratic about Fred Astaire in these roles. (Nobody loves an aristocrat more than do democrats. Recall the ga-ga reception of the late Princess Diana in America, the fuss made when the queen shows up on our shores.) His clothes give him away, and so does his accent. Astaire is above all an aristocrat of talent. Balzac says that a true artist is a prince, and there is a lot to it. The real aristocrats of art are those who make their art look easy. This Astaire did, incomparably. It was a great fraud, of course, since no one worked harder than he to make what he did look easy. But this kind of fraud is at the center of art— may indeed be intrinsic to art.

One of the first rules of American movies, as even the least crass Hollywood producer will be pleased to inform you, is that there must be someone in them for whom the audience can root. We root for Fred Astaire in his movies in good part because he isn't all that sexy. Unlike Clark Gable, he can't ever say that frankly he doesn't give a damn, sweep up the girl in his arms, and carry her up an impressive staircase to get on with the business of delayed rape (*Gone with the Wind*). Unlike Gary Cooper, he can't win the girl through his manly reticence and unflinching courage in the face of danger (*High Noon*). Unlike Cary

Grant, he can't bring off the dazzling talk and brute handsomeness that wins through over the steady affection and great wealth offered by Ralph Bellamy (*His Girl Friday*).

Fred Astaire had none of these things going for him. He was this little guy, skinny, with big ears, a long chin, and too wide a forehead, whose only chance is to get the girl onto the dance floor, where he will let his feet do his seducing for him. And yet root for him we do. We do so because he is almost always coming from behind. Part of Fred Astaire's charm is that in many of his movies he is at least partially an underdog. In the scripts of the movies he appears in, one or another kind of misidentification, bungled opportunity, or other bit of bumbling occurs, which, in the football phrase, gives Astaire very poor field position from which he is under the necessity of making up ground. The point is that if only he can get these lovely women on the dance floor, victory will be his, and everyone will dance happily ever after. (Living with such a jumpy fellow after marriage might be something else, but let that go.)

Once he is on the dance floor, of course, Fred Astaire is no longer an underdog. He becomes, as they say in Vegas, an odds-on, a positively prohibitive favorite. On the dance floor—just him and the night and the music—his charm kicks in, the girl is his, the movie's over, you walk out of the theater (or, more likely nowadays, rise from your couch before the television set), and, humming the flick's final song, wonder why in the hell it wasn't given to you to be able to move as lightly, as wonderfully, as absolutely charmingly as Fred Astaire.

The Other Guy

Hard today to grasp that tap dancing, a minor art now lapsing into a disappearing one, was once not only vastly admired but also widely taught and practiced. In the 1940s, tap dance lessons were offered, for twenty-five cents a shot, in the public schools of Chicago and no doubt in other public school systems. I took them; or, rather, I took one such lesson: shuffle step, step, shuffle step, step, heel toe, heel toe, step, shuffle step, step, step, step. The prospect of tap dancing, at least for this failed hoofer, was much more delightful than the drudgery, the endless repetition, of learning how to do it.

The reason for the popularity of tap dancing at that time was that this minor but genuine art seemed to be everywhere in the movies, and the movies were never more popular than in the 1940s, when ninety million people in a population of a hundred and fifty million in the United States went to the movies at least once a week. The movie musical was also very much a going concern, and most actors, if pressed, seemed able to do a buck-and-wing or a little shuffle-off-to-Buffalo. Lots of actors started their careers as tap dancers—hoofers, in the approved show biz term—George Raft, Jimmy Cagney, Buddy Ebsen, George Murphy, Dan Dailey, and Shirley Temple among them; Barbara Stanwyck entered show business as a teenage tap-dancing chorus girl.

The origin of tap dancing is thought to be African, or, more specifically, African-American. African slaves in America, denied the use of drums, tapped out old tribal rhythms with their feet, or so at least the story goes. Irish clog and jig dancing are also supposed to have contributed to the art. Aluminum taps on the heels and toes of shoes came into being in the early decades of the twentieth century. American blacks were dominant among tap performers, from the nineteenth-century dancer William Henry Lane (1825–52) through Bill Bojangles Robinson (1878–1949), John Bubbles (1902–86), the Nicholas Brothers (Fayard, 1914–2006, and Harold, 1921–2000),

Gregory Hines (1946–2003), through (for now) Savion Glover.

Every performer seemed to have a repertoire of tap-dance steps. And so did Danny Kaye, Dick Powell, Frank Sinatra, Bob Hope, Cary Grant, and a great many others. Sammy Davis, Jr., started out as a child tap dancer with the Will Maston Trio. Ruby Keeler, Ann Miller, Eleanor Powell, Vera-Ellen, Judy Garland were notable among women tap dancers. A gentleman named Henry LeTang, who taught a great many Hollywood figures to tap dance, included among his clients Milton Berle, Harry Belafonte, Lola Falana, Lena Horne, Bette Midler, Flip Wilson, and (picture this, please) Lee Marvin, Clifton Webb, and Lenny Bruce. LeTang also choreographed the movies *The Cotton Club* and *Tap*.

Tap dancing is nothing if not virtuosic, by which ugly and awkward word is meant, not to put too fine a point on it, showing off. Individual routines tend to run to the intricate, the strenuous, or the plain speedy. (A man named Roy Castle, according to the *Guinness Book of World Records*, was able to dance at the rate of fourteen hundred taps a minute, or twenty-four per second.) Splits and backflips in the old tap routines were not uncommon. Soft shoe, or dancing without taps on one's soles, tends to be (naturally) quieter, mellower, as does sand dancing, in which one swishes around in sand strewn on the floor, but here, too, at some point, the spirit of Hey, Yo, Ma, Look, No Hands! kicks in.

The world's greatest tap dancer, from all reports, must have been Bill Bojangles Robinson. He was smooth and beautifully in control while doing astonishing, masterly small subtle bits. He invented something called "the stair dance." Later George Gershwin wrote a song about a dance man titled "I'll Build a Stairway to Paradise," perhaps with Bill Robinson in mind. Robinson once told Astaire, "Boy, you can dance," which was no small praise. Fred Astaire pays tribute to Bill Robinson with a song called "Bojangles of Harlem," a Jerome Kern–Dorothy Fields number, which he sings and to which he beautifully dances, in noncondescending blackface, in the movie *Swing Time*. When Astaire and his sister met Bill Robinson in Harlem in the 1920s, the great master is said to have taught him a new shuffle, six steps up and six steps down, that he would make much use of later in his career.

Donald O'Connor, Ray Bolger, Dan Dailey were other actors whose careers were anchored in their tap dancing. O'Connor and Bolger tap-danced to sweet comic effect; in "Make 'Em Laugh" in *Singin' in the Rain*, the Gene Kelly movie, O'Connor brilliantly captures the pure show-off element in tap dancing in a dance number that is about tap dance as nothing more than pure showing off. Dailey, a burly man for a dancer, was able to play romantic leads. Cagney chiefly tap-danced early in his career, and he did a kind of pure hoofing in which all the activity was in his legs; he did a machine gun–like tapping, jerkily moving sideways across the stage, while the upper part of his body remained almost still. This is on display in *Yankee Doodle Dandy*, in which he played George M. Cohan: "a manic punchinello," the movie critic David Thomson nicely calls him in the role.

The great tap dancer in the movies, along with Fred Astaire, was of course Gene Kelly. People commonly compare and contrast the two dancers, preferring one over the other. Comparisons and contrasts are surely in order, for each dancer highlights the distinctive quality in the other; and rightly so, for in some ways, no two vastly talented dancers could have been more different.

Fred Astaire always played it country-club urbane, even when his part called for his being from Indiana (as in *Roberta*), while Gene Kelly played his roles as the poor kid from the big-city streets. Kelly was thirteen years younger than Astaire. Astaire came to maturity in the booming, jazz-soaked 1920s, Kelly in the Depression-wracked 1930s. Kelly played the common man—the guy on the GI bill trying to paint in Europe (*An American in Paris*), the movie star of working-class origins (*Singin' in the Rain*). Kelly was the dancing (and Irish) analog to (the Jewish) John Garfield—the stocky, handsome guy, touchy, takes no crap from anyone, underneath it all, though, very sensitive. In Astaire movies, crap doesn't arise, touchy never comes into play, and what's sensitive got to do with anything?

In their book *Gene Kelly: A Celebration*, Sheridan Morley and Ruth Leon call Kelly "the man who took dancing out of white tie and tails and set it bubbling on the furnace of street life." Kelly, in fact, set out deliberately to distinguish himself from Astaire. "I tried to be completely different from Astaire," he said. "I had an objection to the kind of dancing I saw on the screen in those days [the 1930s]. There was a lot of great dancing but the trouble was, everybody seemed rich. As a Depression kid who went to school in very tough times, I didn't want to move or dance like a rich man. I wanted to do the dance of the Proletariat, the movements of the people."

As that remark suggests, Gene Kelly was a bit of a left-winger. His first wife, the actress Betsy Blair—she played Ernest Borgnine's girlfriend in *Marty*—was in genuine danger from the congressional Red hunts of the early 1950s for her dalliances with the American Communist

Party, which was, in part, why Kelly moved his family to Europe during those years. In actuality, Astaire grew up in much grimmer conditions than Kelly, who had two parents on the scene, had a perfectly normal middle-class childhood, went for a while to Penn State University, and knew nothing of the asperities of Astaire's childhood of furnished rooms and long train rides between theatrical engagements.

Sartorially, Kelly dressed down: baseball caps, scruffy loafers, and sweat socks, T- and polo shirts, V-neck sweaters, shirts with soft collars worn outside sport jackets. He looked a touch uncomfortable in a necktie, and though he wore white tie and tails on occasion, it never really came off. Astaire, never *not* turned-out, looked dashing even in sweated-out rehearsal clothes. The only article of apparel they had in common was the toupee.

Astaire and Kelly were too much the gents for either to comment in a critical way on the dancing of the other. The two men were not friends—though there was no known enmity between them—but they always spoke respectfully of each other. Kelly's was the younger, more with-it Hollywood set; Astaire's, insofar as he had a set at all, was more traditional, old-line. The English drama critic Kenneth Tynan, originator of the soft-porn Broadway show *Oh! Calcutta!*, might show up at a Gene and

Betsy Kelly party; Astaire would have felt very uncomfortable around a man like Tynan.

Astaire allowed that Kelly was more contemporary in his appeal: "My style no longer matches the contemporary mood," he said, "and I see Gene Kelly now gaining the admiration that greeted me ten years earlier." Kelly remarked on the differences in their two approaches to dance: "Fred's steps were small, neat, graceful and intimate, where mine were ballet-oriented and very athletic." They tended not to be chosen for the same parts in movies, though when Kelly had injured himself playing volleyball at one of his lawn parties, he persuaded Astaire to take over his part and play opposite Judy Garland in *Easter Parade*.

Gene Kelly was artistically more ambitious than Fred Astaire. Often with the aid of Hermes Pan, Astaire choreographed almost all his own movie dance numbers, but Kelly choreographed entire movies (a few with the help of the director Stanley Donen), a couple of which he also directed. "I never was crazy about performing," Kelly said; "even as a dancer I liked to create the stuff, I liked dancing, but I never really worked at the dancing." Astaire was content to be the best possible dancer he could be, while Kelly wanted to change the nature of movie dancing: to integrate dance numbers more smoothly into the plots of films than was done in the Astaire movies; he wanted to make movie musicals radically different from stage musicals, with the greater range and flexibility that the camera allowed. Kelly tried to dance the character he played; Astaire played only one character, fellow name of Fred Astaire, and danced it exquisitely.

Gene Kelly danced with Judy Garland, Leslie Caron, Cyd Charisse, Vera-Ellen, with all of whom Astaire also danced, but Kelly never found his Ginger Rogers. One doesn't think of Kelly as a partnered, or ballroom, dancer, but as a soloist; in John Updike's term he wasn't quite "partnerable." Astaire was both, brilliant soloist and graceful partner, though today he is remembered chiefly for dancing sublimely with women. John Gielgud said that "the best dancers are the best showers-off of a woman." This Fred Astaire did to the greatest extent possible.

The two men were different body types. Both were short, but Astaire, owing to his long legs and slenderness, seemed tall. Gene Kelly was thick in the legs, wide-shouldered, broad-chested, stocky, a powerful running back to Fred Astaire's agile wide receiver. When young, Kelly, who had a Canadian father, was a semipro hockey player. He was muscular and liked to appear on screen with his sleeves rolled up.

As a boy whose mother insisted that he and his brothers and sisters take dancing lessons, Kelly was intent on proving the masculinity of dancing, and spoke out on the point in a public way more than once. He did an *Omnibus* television show with the title "Dancing: A Man's Game." During that show Kelly said: "I think dancing is a man's game, and if a man does it well he does it better than a woman." He fought off the idea that dancing was effeminate, saying that whatever the actual sexuality of the dancer, effeminate dancing was bad dancing. "This stigma on dancing is tragic," he said, "because a great many boys would benefit from dancing lessons. It's the finest kind of exercise and it teaches poise." He then went on to find analogies to dancing in sports: "A quarterback making a forward pass can be as beautiful as a ballet movement, and a double play in baseball, if it's done well, has a choreographic feeling. Boxers, from James J. Corbett to Sugar Ray Robinson, use dancing as part of their art, but, of course, they don't run the risk of being called sissies." For Fred Astaire none of this was an issue.

Gene Kelly played movie roles that were clearly impossible for Astaire. His breakthrough role on the stage was in *Pal Joey*, the John O'Hara story, in which he portrays a heel who uses women to advance his own shabby career. (In the movie, to Kelly's chagrin, Frank Sinatra was asked to play the part.) Fred Astaire playing the role is unimaginable. Astaire didn't do heels, he didn't do creeps. He did frivolous, charming, happy; mean or too dispirited wasn't in his range, was probably even against his nature.

Kelly played pirates and he was D'Artagnan in *The Three Musketeers.* The notion of Fred Astaire in the tights necessary to these parts is preposterous, though my guess is he would have arranged to do the swordfighting bits dashingly. Kelly often played aggressive, chips-on-both-shoulders parts. Kelly's muscularity is always in evidence. (He moved about with his two chips at all times nicely balanced.) In most of his dances we notice Gene Kelly's rear end; in Fred Astaire's case, it's as if his body didn't come equipped with a rear end.

Cyd Charisse, the desolatingly beautiful Cyd Charisse, who danced with both men, said that Kelly was "the more inventive choreographer" but "Astaire's coordination is better," with a sense of rhythm that is "uncanny." Kelly was the stronger of the two men: "When he lifts you, he lifts you! Fred could never do the lifts Gene did and never wanted to." Miss Charisse also remarked, "If I were black and blue after I had [danced with] Gene," "I didn't have a scratch [on me] when it was Fred." She never said directly with which of the two she preferred dancing.

I once asked a beautiful, rather fragile woman, then in her forties, with whom she would rather spend an evening, Fred Astaire or Gene Kelly? "Gene Kelly," she answered. "I would feel more protected with him." Ah, I thought, though did not say, "But in the event of trouble Fred Astaire would have sent you safely off in a cab." But the choice really comes down to whether one's temperament tends to the Apollonian (or classic and understatedly calm, like Astaire) or Dionysian (or romantic with high-banked fires, like Kelly).

Two women who disagreed about Fred Astaire and Gene Kelly are Pauline Kael and Arlene Croce, then, respectively, the movie and dance critics of the *New Yorker*. Ms. Croce found the dancing of Astaire, which seems on the surface less sophisticated, in fact purer, more classical, whereas Kelly's dancing, tied to the plots of the movies in which he danced, caused "the pressure in a dance number . . . often [to] seem too low, the dance itself plebeian or folksy in order to 'match up' with the rest of the picture." Ms. Kael thought Kelly's acting had greater "warmth and range," "even though Kelly isn't a winged dancer; he's a hoofer and more earthbound." Astaire, she thought, "was always and only a light comedian and could function only in fairytale vehicles."

In *The Bandwagon* Fred Astaire, dancing with Cyd Charisse, did a dramatic, sexually charged dance, "The Girl Hunt Ballet," set in a barroom in which he wore a yellow suit, gray fedora, and black shirt. The number resembles a little "Broadway Ballet," which Gene Kelly did with Miss Charisse in *Singin' in the Rain*. Although Astaire does it, for my money, better than Kelly, it nonetheless feels wrong: deep drama and highly charged sexuality were never what Fred Astaire's dancing was about. Hold the *Sturm*, cancel the *Drang*. "Astaire for elegance," the English movie critic Dilys Powell said, "Kelly for command." Gene Kelly himself said: "If I am the Marlon Brando of dancing, Fred Astaire's Cary Grant." That ain't bad.

The two men danced together just once, in the movie *Ziegfeld Follies*. The dance, performed to a dullish Gershwin song called "The Babbitt and the Bromide," is a disappointing little exercise in strained humor. Astaire glides through the number; Kelly makes hard work of it. A few rocky moments occur when the two dancers knock each other's derby hats off and, at one point, kick each other in the pants, suggesting, fleetingly and quite unintentionally, how ugly any open rivalry between them might have been.

As Pauline Kael, comparing the two dancers, once said, "Astaire is impervious to emotion, no matter what the calamity he has to face . . . whereas Kelly is a suffering human being. Kelly bleeds and Astaire doesn't." Yet there is an aggressiveness to Kelly's manner that is not always attractive; and as an actor he did more than the permissible percentage of mugging; often a strong element of show-biz look-at-me-knocking-myself-out corniness shows up in his performances.

The chief difference between Gene Kelly and Fred Astaire as dancers is that Kelly is always stressing the arduousness of what he is doing, while Astaire is dedicated to making it all look easy. Perhaps this is why so many of Gene Kelly's dance numbers seem a little too long, whereas one wishes Fred Astaire's would never stop. Kelly's "Slaughter on Tenth Avenue" and the long ballet he staged at the conclusion of *An American in Paris* qualify as overdramatized, which is perhaps only another way of saying pretentious. Astaire never lapsed into pretension, never had to worry about effeminacy leeching into his dancing, never tried to stop the show with heavy athleticism—never did any of these things, never even came close. Kelly huffed and puffed, Astaire glided and grinned. Final score: Apollo 35, Dionysius 21.

What's It Their Business?

Vast differences there were, too, between the offscreen personalities of Fred Astaire and Gene Kelly. Kelly was aggressive, argumentative, sometimes in the name of good causes, such as his wanting to attempt aesthetic effects in movies that Hollywood producers, in their innate financial conservatism, were nervous about trying. A strong liberal, he was also a more openly political personality than Astaire, who never made his politics known, but whose temperamental disposition was conservative: he was churchgoing, patriotic (he did lots of work entertaining troops during World War II), and dismissive of the new music and the more open sexiness of movies in the seventies.

Few are the stories about Fred Astaire arguing with studio heads and producers, and this is perhaps because he seems generally to have gotten his way. His "way" chiefly meant being permitted much lengthier rehearsal periods than was usual in the Hollywood of that day. Deference was paid to Astaire because his early pictures—*The Gay Divorcee, Roberta, Top Hat*—made huge profits for RKO. He was always considered a valuable property, and treated as such. He had a share in the financial profits of these early films, and, with his wife carefully investing them, became a wealthy man. More than once he announced his retirement from the movies, and more than once tempting offers were made to lure him back to work. He was in the enviable condition of being in demand, beholden to no one, and in a studio system that was often considered high-priced bondage he came as close as one could to being his own man. He also had a clear understanding of how highly he was valued, and that he could cash this in by insisting on his own performance standards. "I'm not interested in doing anything crummy," he once told a television producer.

Apart from in the movies, Fred Astaire never felt much need to display his personality in a public way. He gave few interviews, and those reluctantly. He was fortunate in coming into his prominence at a time before the exposé impulse had arrived in reporting about the movies. He appeared on the *Dick Cavett Show* late in life, where he was treated with great care, fawningly even, never pressed with questions that might have caused him discomfort. He had done an Edward R. Murrow *Person to Person* interview earlier, and here, too, no attempt was made to swim into deep, let alone murky, waters. "Tell us about those drums in your room, if you please, Mr. Astaire" was about as deep as Murrow chose to go.

Astaire, meanwhile, specialized in gainsaying his achievements. "I'm just a hoofer," he'd say. Or "I made a pretty good buck," he'd say. At the American Film Institute tribute to him, when his friend and sometimes co-choreographer Hermes Pan spoke about having just returned from Italy, where he had found the love of the Italians for Fred Astaire, who seemed to embody all that was best about America, Astaire, from his table, made a shooing gesture with his hand, as if to say, "Knock that crap off, please." After watching an hour's clips of many of the best bits from his movie dancing, he remarked that some of it wasn't at all bad, then went on to say that his sister Adele had the talent in the family and he had just gone along for the ride. All baloney, of course, but it was the way he operated: he knew how good he was, and therefore felt no need for self-promotion. He ended the

American Film Institute evening on a not very impressive response to the vast quantity of praise given him by haltingly noting that it was getting awfully late.

People today are known to say, "I'm a very private person." Usually they say it in the most public places: on, for example, television talk shows. Fred Astaire, though, genuinely valued his privacy. In *Easter Parade*, the movie he made with Judy Garland, Miss Garland's character Hannah Brown tells Jonathan Harrow III (Peter Lawford) of the Astaire character, Don Hewes, "He never talks about himself. Just about dancing. Everything's strictly business." And so it was in Astaire's life.

He lived mainly within his family: with his wife, his wife's son (Peter), his own son (Fred, Jr.) and his daughter (Ava). He golfed, he gardened, he bought a few racehorses. He seemed to have little appetite for Hollywood parties; getting him to come to one's party was always thought a bit of coup for the hostess. He had no known—and, my guess is, no unknown—love affairs while married to Phyllis.

He guarded his personal life carefully and felt no need to allow strangers, which meant journalists, entrée to it. This didn't stop them from trying. Notable among them was Helen Lawrenson, a woman who, like Fred Astaire, came of age in the 1920s and who is probably best known, if she is any longer known at all, as the author of an *Esquire* article called "Latins Make Lousy Lovers," an article in the magazine *Swank* called "Why Nice Girls Abandon Underwear," and the remark that "whatever else can be said about sex, it cannot be called a dignified performance." A specialist in the brash, a straight shooter with her gun always aimed at the tenderest of places, Ms. Lawrenson was not quite, as you will have gathered, Fred Astaire's notion of a jolly good time.

Helen Lawrenson's interview with the seventy-seven-year-old Fred Astaire ran in the August 1977 issue of *Esquire*, though noninterview may come closer to describing the proceedings. Lawrenson begins by remarking upon how, like everyone else, she is enraptured by Astaire's dancing. But she quickly gets down to a slight testiness on the matter of his being known as the man who misses the party: "He was invited everywhere and went nowhere." She follows this up by noting what she takes to be his Anglophiliac snobbery. At a party at the Waldorf in the 1930s, Tallulah Bankhead told Lawrenson that Fred Astaire never went anywhere, "except with the ritzy titled set." In America, Lawrenson informs us, he ran with the Whitneys and Vanderbilts. Ms. Lawrenson was herself a person interested in left-wing causes, so Astaire's hobnobbing with the very wealthy cannot be a good thing.

Helen Lawrenson, as we shall see, turned out to be one of those people, found on left and right both, who feel that if you do not share their political views, you may not quite deserve to be put to death, but something, clearly, is deeply defective in you.

Ms. Lawrenson mentions to her readers that she has arrived at her room at the Beverly Wilshire reflecting on the fact that Fred Astaire does not enjoy interviews. Newspaper friends have warned her that he was "'boring and grumpy' and that Hollywood columnists long ago placed him high on their lists of least-cooperative stars." Still, Ms. Lawrenson is not without her own charms, and is confident that she can break through any resistance he might offer.

When Lawrenson arrives at Astaire's Beverly Hills house, she notes the three cars in his garage, one of them a Rolls-Royce, black with bright turquoise leather uphol-stery. "Nice," she writes, "but a mite gaudy, like the leopard-skin print on the armchairs in his big living room." No books in sight, either, except bound volumes of the *Racing Form* and scripts from Astaire's own movies. She also thinks him perhaps a little too neatly turned out: "A little too perfect, too dapper. I think the word is 'natty.'" By now a careful reader will realize that Fred Astaire isn't going to have an easy time with Ms. Lawrenson.

She, on the other hand, probably would say that she didn't have such a hot time with him, either. She begins by querying Astaire about the unusual circumstance of his mother taking him and his sister from Omaha off to New York at such an early age. "I don't want to talk about it," he says. She asks about his father, what he did, how it was he allowed his children to go off to New York without him? He doesn't want to talk about that, either. Nor is he forthcoming on the subject of horse racing. "Stop looking at your watch," she tells him. "I can't leave until the MGM man comes back to get me."

At some point in every encounter of a celebrity with a journalist the reader has to choose sides. (True, many are the instances in which it is difficult to choose, so closely are one's antipathies divided.) In this particular encounter, I found myself entirely on Fred Astaire's side. Why, after all, need he accommodate Helen Lawrenson? And of what would accommodation consist? Spilling all the beans, no doubt. Telling her that his mother was a monster, his father a ne'er do well, that he made a nice little bundle on the ponies, that Ginger Rogers was terrible in the sack, nothing like so exciting as Rita Hayworth. And even if he had wild or searing stories to tell, why divulge them to Ms. Lawrenson, who would only move on to attempt to dig up more dirt for yet another story for her next assignment?

Fred Astaire has many unpredictable admirers, and among them was the tough-guy Chicago journalist Mike Royko, not a man one easily imagines dancing cheek to cheek with anyone but a grizzly bear. But Royko turns out to have loved everything about Astaire, including his walk: "He could stroll across a room with more style than most dancers can dance." More to the point, at Astaire's death, Royko, in his *Chicago Tribune* and syndicated column, wrote: "As the years went on, I found something else about him I admired tremendously. It was that I knew very little about him, other than what I saw on the screen. . . . I didn't read about his love life or about his punching somebody in a nightclub. I didn't read about him storming off a set, feuding with a director, fighting with the press or babbling about what he liked to eat, what he liked to drink, snort, or smoke. . . . In other words, he did his work, went home, closed the door, and said: 'That's it, world. You get my performance. The rest belongs to me.'"

The rest of the Helen Lawrenson interview is devoted to whittling Fred Astaire down further. She suggests that Astaire and Ginger Rogers hated each other. She speculates that, between Fred and his sister Adele, it was Adele who was the great natural dancer on whom audiences most ardently fastened. She quotes him in some snobbish twaddle about knowing the current queen of England when she was an infant. As she at last leaves, she says to him, "That wasn't so bad, was it?" He doesn't reply.

Ms. Lawrenson then goes off to Gene Kelly's, where she gets a warmer welcome. Kelly asks if she would like something to eat or drink. "Fred," she notes, "hadn't even offered a glass of water." (Fortunately, one feels, she didn't ask to use the bathroom at Astaire's.) Kelly doesn't exactly put Astaire down—he says in fact that Astaire's will be the only dancing of the day to be remembered fifty years later—but tells her that Astaire had no interest in coming to the Kellys', where Judy Garland and Frank Sinatra often hung out, preferring instead the company of the very rich and the titled.

Helen Lawrenson winds up her article by remarking that Astaire's autobiography, *Steps in Time*, which he suggested she read, is so dull as to put her to sleep, speculates that the childhood of the Astaires must have been ghastly, and ends by recounting how pleased Fred was when she told him that Marcello Mastroianni was a great admirer of the Astaire-Rogers movies. But then she cannot help telling us, her readers, in the final sentence of her article, "In truth, what Marcello [note the nice first-name name drop] told me was that he saw all the Astaire-Rogers pictures over and over because he had a crush on Ginger."

She doesn't leave Fred Astaire much, Ms. Lawrenson—doesn't leave him anything at all, really.

What if Helen Lawrenson's portrait of Fred Astaire is accurate? If Astaire at seventy-seven—or even at thirty-two—was dull and guarded about his personal life, how much would it matter? Not, I think, a great deal. Another possibility that Helen Lawrenson failed to consider is that Fred Astaire was shy and not very articulate. Around the same time as the Lawrenson interview, he appeared on Dick Cavett's television show. Astaire's unease even with the admiring Cavett is painful to watch. He sat on the edge of his chair much of the time. Cavett, as was his wont with the famous, slathered him with praise, which Astaire pooh-poohed. He didn't look good, either. He wore a bad toupee, and his eyes looked slightly glazed. He was in his late seventies. His speech was halting and faltering. He said nothing clever or in the least memorable; he bordered, in fact, on the inarticulate. One felt sorry for him. Then, as had pretty clearly been rehearsed, Cavett "persuaded" him to sing some Gershwin, then some Berlin, then some Cole Porter songs, all of which he did wonderfully well. He even did a sweet little dance, a riff of a sort. A pure performer, Astaire scarcely existed outside the realm of performance.

Fred Astaire was the world's wittiest dancer; it's inconceivable, really, that his conversation could have equaled his physical movements—inconceivable that it would have and okay that it didn't. Few are the amusing or penetrating Fred Astaire remarks: most of what he said for public consumption is flat and rather obvious. All his brilliant sayings had been enunciated by his feet. I find myself admiring his reticence before journalists. It's his life, as my dear mother might have said, what's it their business?

Who Needs a Partner?

Beaumont and Fletcher, Laurel and Hardy, Abbott and Costello, Rodgers and Hart—Fred and Ginger qualify as another of these famous pairings, with one proviso. Although in their splendid movie performances they never gave any sign of it, neither was entirely content to be linked with the other. Astaire felt he had had the great partnership of his career with his sister Adele; and Ginger Rogers, though hers would probably by now be a less luminous name but for her partnership with Fred Astaire, sensed that he somehow eclipsed her; what's more, she wished to be thought, more than a mere dancer, a great actress.

At the 1988 Democratic Convention, Ann Richards, soon to be governor of Texas, said that on the dance floor,

Ginger Rogers had done everything that Fred Astaire did, but "backwards and in high heels." Katharine Hepburn remarked that to the Fred-and-Ginger partnership Rogers brought sex and Astaire brought class, the combination thought to provide a winning mix. A strange word *class*, one always to be suspicious of, especially in a democracy, which is officially dedicated to eliminating all evidence of social class. What the baggy-pants word *class* usually means is style on an upper-class level of elegance, and sometimes it can be applied to an act of generosity suggesting a noble spirit. Ann Richards's and Katharine Hepburn's are interesting remarks, but how high is the quotient of truth in either one?

Tension was never quite missing from the Fred-Ginger relationship, even though both Astaire and Rogers, putting the best face on things, often pretended otherwise. He was twelve years older than she, and they began before their Hollywood days as, potentially, what the gossip columnist Walter Winchell would have termed an item. After being called in to offer choreographic advice on a Broadway show Rogers was in, Astaire, then in his man-about-town bachelor phase, later phoned her for a date. He was also in a show at the time, and he picked her up at midnight for dinner at the Casino, one of those smart supper clubs of the day, where Eddy Duchin's orchestra played. They danced, and he passed the test as a social dancer: "You could put yourself in his hands and trust to his feet," she said. A chauffeur was driving his Rolls-Royce town car, and the evening ended on a kiss that "would never have passed the Hays Office code!" according to Ginger Rogers in her autobiography. "If I had stayed in New York, I think Fred Astaire and I might have become a more serious item," she writes. "We were different in some ways but alike in others. Both of us were troupers from an early age [she was born Virginia McMath of Missouri and moved at an early age to Texas by her gila monster (those ferocious lizards said never to let go) of a stage mother], both of us loved a good time, and, for sure, both of us loved to dance." In the account in Astaire's autobiography, they went out on dates a few more times, but there was neither spark nor fan to flame it.

When they were assigned to do their first picture together, *Flying Down to Rio*, in which both had second-banana roles, much had changed: Ginger Rogers had appeared in a few movies, and Fred Astaire, now married and without his sister Adele as his partner, had determined on a career in the movies. She felt that "Fred looked the same but acted differently. He was not as open, far more formal." This was owing, she thought, to his new wife, who, in her view, made everyone uncomfortable. "One thing's for sure, she [Phyllis Astaire] never warmed up to me . . . and she surely didn't want her husband to either. Other than on the dance floor, Fred and I rarely embraced in our films. Fred said he couldn't stand mushy love scenes and felt like a fool kissing for the camera. Frankly, I think Phyllis didn't want him kissing other women." Henceforth in her autobiography, Ginger Rogers's account of her relationship with Fred Astaire will be by no means barbed but, somehow, less than fully appreciative. In his autobiography, he refers to her as "Gin," but his treatment of her and of their partnership is generally cool, more than a touch distant.

Always the perfectionist, Astaire liked to have a say in the selection of his partners' dresses, chiefly to see whether they were dresses that "danced well," by which he meant flowed and didn't go against the rhythmic grain of the dances he and Hermes Pan had devised. The first time this became a problem was in *Top Hat*, for the dance to the Irving Berlin song "Cheek to Cheek." Ginger Rogers chose a dress covered with blue ostrich feathers. Astaire thought the dress a serious mistake. According to David Niven, who was at the studio that day, Phyllis, who had a tough time pronouncing her r's, said, "She looks like a wooster." Mark Sandrich, who directed many of the early Fred and Ginger movies at RKO, attempted to get her to change her dress. It was nonnegotiable. "Fred didn't like the dress," she writes. "That was the root of the problem." She called in her mother to defend her position. "Why don't you just get another girl," her mother told Sandrich.

The show, as it invariably and usually rather boringly does, went on. "It's true," Ginger Rogers writes, "some of the feathers did flutter and annoy Fred." Astaire's account of the great featherdress episode has feathers flying all over the joint: "Everything went well through the song, but when we did the first movement of the dance, feathers started to fly as if a chicken had been attacked by a coyote." In Rogers's version, a few loose feathers adhered to Astaire's suit coat. In Astaire's version, "It was like a snow-storm. They were floating around like millions of moths. I had feathers in my eyes, my ears, my mouth, all over the front of my suit, which just happened to be a white-tie-and-tails outfit." That was a first take. Things, according to Astaire, didn't improve all that much on further takes.

Then there was the dance with the beaded dress with bell sleeves Ginger Rogers wore to dance to "Let's Face the Music and Dance" in *Follow the Fleet*. "Fred had to face a little music concerning my dress, too," she writes, for her sleeves slapped against his jaw when she whirled, and continued to do so after several takes. In Astaire's account, in each of twenty different takes he took blows to the jaw and eye, and all he could do was keep "ducking and dodging that sleeve."

Pandro S. Berman, the producer of most of the RKO Astaire-Rogers movies, claimed that Ginger Rogers's wardrobe was a continuing problem. "Whenever Fred came to me to register a complaint about her appalling taste in gowns her mother would jump into the fray and we'd have a real Donnybrook."

Things were made more complicated by Ginger Rogers's feeling that she wasn't getting the attention she deserved from Sandrich. On other occasions she complained that Astaire was the central figure, once calling a dopey song, "The Yam," that she was assigned in the movie *Carefree* as "another hand-me-down from Fred." She remarks on how much more money Astaire made on the RKO musicals than she. Although she attempts to downplay it, what comes through in Ginger Rogers's autobiography is that in the Astaire-Rogers partnership she, a much more beautiful Rodney Dangerfield, didn't get no respect.

She may have been right. Tim Satchell, one of Fred Astaire's biographers, claims that Astaire "knew very well that Ginger Rogers was a champion Charleston hoofer and was a hard-working professional but not for a second did he consider her to be anywhere near the kind of partner that he wanted or needed: she simply didn't have the dance technique to match his." Hermes Pan said: "Their rhythms were just different. I wouldn't decry Ginger as a dancer. She is truly wonderful, but [with] a totally different style to Fred." Yet she learned his style, copied it fairly exactly in many of their tap-dance numbers together, and danced with him more harmoniously than any of his other partners.

Perfectionist is another word for great worrier, and Fred Astaire probably over-rehearsed, which meant that his partners had to rehearse quite as much as he did. He appears to have worked Ginger Rogers hardest of all. Talk was bruited about of her bleeding feet. Her work on the Astaire-Rogers movies, she says, was "murder for me. Oh, I adored Mr. A. but all the hard work ... the 5 A.M. calls, the months of non-stop dancing [in rehearsals], singing and acting." Granting that she hung in there, Astaire allows that "she had guts."

In her autobiography, Ginger Rogers mentions Astaire's displays of temperament on the set while simultaneously saying that he wasn't very temperamental. She retells an anecdote about his losing his cool when his top hat fell off in the filming of the movie *Top Hat*, revealing that he had neglected to wear his toupe—in other words, she dings him whenever possible. He in turn always writes with what one feels is a slightly strained courtesy about her. But, one notices by way of contrast, he seems frequently to compliment the dancing of other partners—Eleanor Powell, Rita Hayworth, Judy Garland—more than he does hers. At the American Film Institute award in his honor, conspicuous by her absence among the people offering tributes to him was Ginger Rogers. Which was, apparently, all right with Astaire. She was hurt not to have been invited. According to Tim Satchell, "Astaire had let it be known that he would rather that she was not present—otherwise the great scene-stealer would undoubtedly have done something dramatic."

The not so plain fact seems to be that, however much American moviegoers loved them together, however earnestly each tried to put the best face on things, Fred Astaire and Ginger Rogers, without despising each other, probably did not all that much like each other either. Although their social class origins were not so very different, he had climbed higher in the world than she, and she may have felt that he, with his socialite wife, his Anglophiliac manner and style, looked down on her. She was over-, he under-, stated. She was pure show biz, which is to say gaudy, in a way that he, though in show business all his life, somehow avoided being.

Neither much liked the notion of being subsumed as part of a team: Astaire had already done that with his sister; Rogers thought of herself as much more than a mere dancer (she did, after all, go on to win an Oscar for her role in *Kitty Foyle*), and doubtless sensed that, good as the two of them were together, Fred Astaire somehow outshone her. Astaire even wrote to Leland Hayward, his agent, after the success of *The Gay Divorcee*, that he wished never again to be part of a fixed team in his movie career, and especially not with Ginger Rogers:

What's all this talk about being teamed with Ginger Rogers? I will *not* have it Leland—I did not go into pictures to be *teamed* with her or anyone else, and if that is the program in mind for me I will not stand for it. I don't mind making another picture with her but as for this *team* idea it's *out!* I've just managed to live down one partnership and I don't want to be bothered with any more. I'd rather not make any more pictures for Radio [RKO] if I have to be teamed up with one of those movie "queens." This is no flash of temperament on my part Leland and does not call for one of your famous bawling out letters—please understand that. I'm just against the idea—that's all and feel that if I'm ever to get anywhere on the screen it will be as *one* not as two.

Astaire even had a contract drawn up with a clause that Ginger Rogers could not appear in more than three of the five movies he had signed on to do for RKO. In fact, they eventually did ten movies together; in their last of nine at RKO, *The Story of Vernon and Irene Castle*, Mrs. Castle, who had a right of control over the movie and who disliked Ginger Rogers, claimed that "Fred has begged me not to let her do it," though no one can say for certain whether this story is true.

The relative longevity of their partnership is explained by their popularity as a team, which translated into heavy profits. The success of the early Astaire-Rogers movies— *The Gay Divorcee, Roberta, Top Hat, Swing Time*—was said to have been the single reason behind the financial rescue of RKO Studios. As a team they were long at or near the top of various popularity polls for movie stars. Astaire drew a salary of $100,000 for the earlier of his movies with Ginger Rogers and had a share in the gross, which made him a rich man. Money and fame are not bad reasons to bury tensions or even hide complicated feelings. Still, can actors completely fake charm of the kind that

Fred Astaire and Ginger Rogers combined to exude in the marvelous movies they made together?

My guess is that they can fake it, and that Astaire and Rogers did so supremely well. It's called being a pro. Many are the theories of acting—Stanislavsky's, the Actors Studio's, to name only the more modern—but an older theory of acting, one devised by Denis Diderot, the Enlightenment writer and editor of the great French *Encyclopédie*, holds that the truly superior actor, far from feeling more than the rest of us, far from being able to delve into the well of his deep feeling when it is required by his art, the truly superior actor actually feels nothing. In his *Paradox of the Actor*, Diderot writes: "It is extreme sensibility which makes a mediocre actor; mediocre sensibility which makes the multitude of bad actors; and a total lack of sensibility which produces sublime actors." The feeling man or woman, in other words, is likely to be the less successful artist. Feeling gets in the way; it isn't finally what the art of acting is primarily about.

Where Fred Astaire always spoke of his movie roles as just a job, humdrum, a way to make "a pretty good buck," was he being modest? Or was he, as a great artist, of a limited but genuine kind, being entirely truthful? My guess is that he was being truthful. He acted the part it was given him to act, and at the end of the day, like a good artisan, packed up his tools and returned home. The feeling in his performances was not displayed in the mostly inane dialogue that was written for him but in his dancing. He didn't have to love, or even be in any way emotionally engaged with, the woman he was dancing with at the moment. He was instead dedicated to making her look good, which almost inevitably resulted in making himself look even better. He might feel a mild disdain for Ginger Rogers, and she in turn more than a touch of resentment toward him, without its in the least getting in the way of their dazzling performance before the camera. Now that is show business.

Change Partners

Arlene Croce, author of the excellent *The Fred Astaire and Ginger Rogers Book*, underscores the point that Ginger Rogers was as eager to leave the Astaire-Rogers partnership as was Fred Astaire. Rogers thought herself, rightly, a performer of wider talent than was made use of in her movies with Astaire: talent as a dramatic actress, an ingénue, a solo comedienne, all going to waste. She feared—rightly, again—being smothered under Astaire's brilliance.

Owing to Astaire's perfectionism, which required weeks and weeks, sometimes months, of rehearsals before a movie could be shot, Ginger Rogers couldn't take on as many new projects as other female stars among her glittering contemporaries, who included Katharine Hepburn, Myrna Loy, Carole Lombard, Claudette Colbert, Joan Crawford, and Irene Dunne. Besides, the billing was always Astaire-Rogers, never Rogers-Astaire. Hers was not just the last but, really, the secondary name in the partnership, and everybody knew it.

For his part, Fred Astaire wanted to be Fred Astaire, without being lashed to a hyphen connected to someone else's name. Both Astaire and Rogers, then, had their own motives for wanting to separate. Pandro Berman, producer of the RKO Astaire-Rogers musicals—the early ones, the serious winners at the box office—reported having to all but force the two of them to keep the partnership intact for further films.

The complex irony of all this is that Ginger Rogers did better without Fred Astaire than Astaire did without Rogers, and yet in the end Astaire is everywhere taken as having had the greater talent, which as a dancer he clearly did, and the greater career, which he also did. True, Rogers won her Oscar without Astaire; she had a great success in *Stage Door*, with Katharine Hepburn as a costar; she made many more movies than he did. Ginger Rogers without Astaire did all right, and even better than all right. Yet Fred Astaire, good as he always was, except when hamstrung by a script beyond the normal stupidity, was never quite so good as he was in the Fred-and-Ginger movies. Although every expert in movie musicals allows that there have been dancers in Hollywood superior to Ginger Rogers, although Fred Astaire went on to dance in the movies with the best among them, he never found a partner anywhere near so well suited to him as this woman who hadn't had much in the way of training as a dancer and whom he didn't much like.

Astaire made two musicals with the beautiful Rita Hayworth. A trained dancer, a pro, the daughter of Eduardo and Volga Cansino, Spanish dancers whom Astaire knew from his days in vaudeville and much admired, Rita Hayworth was twenty years younger than Fred Astaire when they made *You'll Never Get Rich*, the first of their two movies together. At 5-foot-6 she was almost too tall for him. As a dance technician, she presented no problems: she could do the sumptuous ballroom dance with great glamorous suavity or the jitterbug tap numbers with lavas of energy and appealing ingenuity. "She of course knew," Astaire wrote in his autobiography, "through experience what this dancing business was all about," which for him, given his characteristically laconic manner, is high praise.

And yet, good as they looked from the middle distance on the dance floor, something was missing. They weren't quite believable as a couple. Rita Hayworth was too cool, too remote; everything about her suggested that she couldn't truly be in love with a man like Fred Astaire. She was a woman who could be stimulated only by real worthlessness or rich villainy in a man: she required as paramours tough gamblers (Glenn Ford) or wealthy Nazi sympathizers (Claude Rains), cold criminals (George Macready) or rootless romantics (Orson Welles, to whom she was married between 1943 and 1948). Rita Hayworth needed, in other words, to play off a man she could betray for high stakes; a dangerous man, tempestuous, someone possessive and violent, as likely to slap her around as to make steamy love to her.

Fred Astaire did not meet this job description. In his movie persona Astaire is delightful, Astaire is light, Astaire is a sweetheart. He doesn't slap women around (more likely, by mistake they slap him around)—he brings them flowers, sings to them from the courtyard, dances them into love with him, at the close proposes marriage to them in a slightly stuttering way. Fred Astaire is charming, not sexy, except as sex is transmitted— subtly, sweetly—through charm, which of course it can indubitably be.

In *Broadway Melody of 1940*, Astaire, working now at Metro-Goldwyn-Mayer, was teamed with Eleanor Powell, another professional dancer of great polish who was at the time MGM's main dancing attraction. Astaire was complimentary about her, writing that Miss Powell "certainly rates as one of the all-time great dancing girls." Yet the two somehow never clicked. Eleanor Powell may have been a touch too masculine for Astaire. "She 'put 'em down' like a man," he said, "and really knocked out a tap dance in a class by herself." But there was something straight-up, hard-edged, a little unyielding in her dancing posture, what the dance critics call her "line." Astaire needed someone to share the joyousness of his tap numbers and someone ready to be seduced by his long, lush, whirling, swirling, swooping ballroom dances. Eleanor Powell, essentially a soloist, was not that dancer.

At no point in *Broadway Melody of 1940* is it possible to believe in Fred Astaire and Eleanor Powell as lovers. "A major defect of the film is the near absence of romantic impetus," wrote the splendid dance critic John Mueller.

> Whatever is going on between Astaire and Powell is left to the imagination more than revealed to the eye and ear of the beholder. . . . Although they talk and dance together a great deal during the . . . film, their romance never seems more than perfunctory and mechanical. Astaire must not have been able to

bring himself to feign genuine attraction, even in the dances, to the stiff and steely-grinned Powell, a problem he had with only a few partners in his career. Accordingly, his duets with her, while clever and eventful, tend to be dispassionate displays of virtuosity, and the dancers rarely touch or look at each other. It was decidedly not an artistic marriage made in heaven, and the pair never made another motion picture.

Paulette Goddard, who was the female lead in *Second Chorus*, Fred Astaire's next Gingerless movie, was never advertised as a dancer, and in the film she does a single dance with Astaire to the tune of "I Ain't Hep to That Step, But I'll Dig It." Astaire essentially steers her though the dance; they seem to be holding hands or in each other's arms throughout, as if Miss Goddard might not survive if he let her loose for a second. The movie was slammed critically, and Astaire himself called it "the worst film I ever made," a judgment in which I believe he was correct.

The plot of *Second Chorus* revolves around the rivalry between two aging (because they intentionally flunk out) college trumpeters, Astaire and a thoroughly disagreeable Burgess Meredith, both competing for a job playing trumpet with Artie Shaw's band. The only memorable thing about the movie is that at one point Astaire is allowed to lead the band, trumpet in hand, and while doing so he spins off into an energetic dance solo. In this he anticipates all those serious symphonic conductors—Leonard Bernstein perhaps most famous among them—podium exhibitionists, whom Pierre Boulez has called "those good dancers," by which, you may be sure, he intended no compliment.

Astaire's next partner was the now forgotten Joan Leslie in a movie called *The Sky's the Limit*. Here Astaire plays a Flying Tigers air force ace who leaves a heroes' tour of the United States out of boredom with the adulation he receives. He abandons his uniform and buys boots and a ten-gallon hat, which, atop his slender body, looks more like two hundred litres. He steps into a bar and notes Miss Leslie's Joan Manion, having a drink with her boss, who turns out to be, of all people, Robert Benchley as Phil Harriman.

The plots of Fred Astaire musicals, as we have noted, tend to divide between the mildly ridiculous and the entirely moronic. *The Sky's the Limit* falls into the latter category. In it Astaire's character, imaginatively named Fred, stalks Joan, who is a photographer working for a celebrity gossip magazine of which Harriman is the editor. He follows her, he walks her home, he moves into an apartment adjoining hers. She wakes the next morning to find him in her kitchen, where he has prepared her breakfast. She tries to find him work, not realizing that he is a war hero scheduled soon to return to battle. Plausibility, it is said, is the morality of fiction, which means that this movie ought to do heavy time on a morals charge.

Astaire does a spectacular drunken dance, on a bar, to "One for My Baby," which results in the breakage of much glass. He also does the one completely failed movie dance of his entire career: pretending to be a snake charmer atop a small table in a USO club. Astaire does two dances with Joan Leslie, the final one, to the music of "This Will Be My Shining Hour," on another of those immense terraces that figure in so many of his movies: the terraces are of course dance floors by other means, which explains their immensity. But she is a bit too bulky for him, especially in the shoulders and upper body; and she is without comedic intelligence. (To take up the ample comic slack, Robert Benchley does a brilliant spoof of a talk introducing an after-dinner speaker that is miles beyond the intellectual range of the rest of the script.) At one point, early in the movie, when Miss Leslie tells Astaire about the kind of harmless gossip that she reports on, he notes, in a little not-so-inside joke, "Ginger Rogers and friend."

Another partner problem arises in *The Sky's the Limit:* when the movie was made, Joan Leslie was only seventeen and Fred Astaire was forty-four. This discrepancy in age does not, somehow, ruin the movie—the screenwriters were pretty much able to accomplish this on their own—but from here on Astaire began to worry about seeming too old for his partners.

Vera-Ellen, another Astaire partner, was, unlike Paulette Goddard or Joan Leslie, a professional dancer and as such technically solid. She and Astaire made two movies together, *Three Little Words* and *The Belle of New York.* They should, theoretically, have been fine as a team, but they are instead merely okay. In fact, *The Belle of New York* is one of the few Fred Astaire movies to lose money, not that that necessarily coincides with artistic failure (though in this case it does).

Three Little Words is about the songwriting team of Burt Kalmar and Harry Ruby, and fairly early in it Astaire marries the woman played by Vera-Ellen, which is probably a mistake, for the comedy of romance, which is the specialty of most Astaire movies, disappears as soon as the leading couple marry. Astaire, who plays Burt Kalmar, the lyricist of the team, shares the movie with an unusually subdued Red Skelton, who plays Harry Ruby. The result is that there is altogether too little dancing in the movie. And what dancing there is is less than inspired.

The Belle of New York is a precursor to *Guys and Dolls*, only here instead of a gambler a hopeless rich playboy (Astaire) falls in love with Salvation Army–like worker (Vera-Ellen). In the end, shocking to report, he wins her over. Astaire was fifty-two when the movie was made, a bit old for a playboy, and twenty-two years older than his leading lady. But that isn't the problem. Neither are the dance numbers, which take up fully half of the eighty-one-minute movie: usually the more dancing, the better the movie, Q.E.D. Some of these numbers are in fact spectacular, among them one in which Astaire, recognizing his love for Vera-Ellen, leaves the ground and floats up atop the arch at Washington Square in Greenwich Village, on the outer ledges of which he dances serenely. He also does a brilliant sand-dance to "I Wanna Be a Dancin' Man," which Bob Fosse, a devoted admirer of Astaire, would later do as a tribute to his precursor.

No, the problem in *The Belle of New York* is with the Astaire–Vera-Ellen combination. Although she is meant to play her part as a prig, her irrepressible sweetness keeps breaking through. She resembles nothing so much as a cheerleader before the age when cheerleaders bared their navels and wiggled their bottoms. The absence of aesthetic tension when she and Astaire dance is palpable. (Judy Garland was the first choice for the Vera-Ellen part. Miss Garland was also supposed to have the lead female parts in two other Astaire movies: *Royal Wedding* and *The Barkleys of Broadway*. Health problems were the reason given for her not doing any of these movies; "health problems" being a euphemism, sadly, for pills and drinking and nervous breakdown.) Energy, wit, the convincing pretense of trying to hold back obvious attraction, the things Ginger Rogers seemed to do so well, are missing in Vera-Ellen when she dances with Fred Astaire, and all the technique in the world cannot make up for them.

Astaire had even worse luck with Betty Hutton, with whom he made a single movie, *Let's Dance* (1950), a flick that never really gets going and then finishes badly. The few dances that they do together are chiefly comic ones; in one they dress up as seedy cowboys, kicking each other in the pants, and at one point Ms. Hutton has Astaire on her back and does what the wrestlers call a body spin with him—not a good idea. In speech, in song, in acting generally, Betty Hutton did only *fortissimo, molto rumore*—strong with lots of noise. Everything about the movie is loud. The plot has Astaire as Donald Elwood, a nightclub entertainer who longs to be a business genius, trying to reunite with Kitty McNeil (Hutton), an old love who left him to marry into a Boston Brahmin family. When they meet again, she is widowed with a son played by an exceedingly irritating child actor of the kind that Hollywood in those years seemed to turn out in large numbers. The songs, by Frank Loesser, do not really sing well and are not easily danced to.

Betty Hutton was not a talentless woman, but such talent as she had didn't mesh at all with Fred Astaire's. She is agitated where he is calm, vastly overstated where he tends to the quietly understated. Hers is an unsubtle face, with insufficient play in it to have much range; and her body is chunky, with legs thick at the calves and too ample a *derrière* to give the feeling of lightness and fluidity Astaire required in a partner. She was, essentially, a comedienne, brash division: *Annie Get Your Gun* and all that. But everything about *Let's Dance* is boisterous, not least the five- or six-year-old actor named Gregory Moffett, who plays her son, and who, if the gods be just, will by now have sold more than three thousand used cars in the San Fernando Valley.

The movie ends with Astaire and Hutton riding off in a gondola entering a tunnel of love: all confusions put to rest, all conflicts settled, they will marry. Hard, though, to imagine Astaire, or any other man, finding much joy in a marriage to Miss Hutton. Throughout the movie one almost hopes that Fred Astaire will find a way out of his relationship with this hoydenish woman. As it is, the ending, to a person of imagination with the least sense of the future, is almost a tragedy.

Royal Wedding, Astaire's next movie, is thought to have been based loosely on his own early life, when he and his sister Adele were acclaimed by London theater audiences. Fifty-one years old when he made the movie, he plays the part of a successful brother-and-sister song-and-dance act, the Bowens; Jane Powell plays his sister (modeled, presumably, on Adele Astaire, though without the amusing obscenities). In the movie Ellen Bowen marries an English nobleman (as Adele had), played by Peter Lawford. The problem presented to the screenwriters was to find a romantic interest for Astaire. They did so by linking him with an Englishwoman, a member of the chorus in the show in which he and his sister are the stars. This role is played by the stately Sarah Churchill, the second daughter of Winston Churchill, who, in her refinement, is an anti–Betty Hutton. Astaire dances with Miss Churchill only briefly.

Most of the dancing Astaire does in *Royal Wedding*— the historical backdrop giving the movie its title is the upcoming wedding in London of Queen Elizabeth and

Prince Philip—is with Jane Powell. Noted for her singing, Miss Powell turns out to be an energetic and far from inept dancer, who is especially strong on comedy numbers. Since she and Astaire are playing brother and sister in the movie, there is no need for them to do romantic dances together. That there was a twenty-nine-year difference in age between them was, as we nowadays say, a bit of a stretch, even for a brother and sister, but this difference in age isn't the problem.

The problem is that Jane Powell was eight inches shorter than Fred Astaire, which would make her 4-foot-11 or five foot at best. This made it easier for him to lift her, but it ruined the line of their dances. She was just too small even for the less than large Astaire. When they dance together, it looks as if he is dancing with a twelve-year-old daughter.

What everyone seems to remember from this movie is the famous solo in which Astaire dances on the walls and ceiling of his hotel room, a camera trick that was brought off by his dancing in a rotating cylindrical structure with the furniture and camera nailed to the floor, so that the cameraman and not Astaire was really upside down. Some people like the gum-chewing comic number with Astaire and Powell sung to "How Could You Believe Me When I Said I Love You, When You Know I've Been a Liar All

My Life," but then, with the exception of his two-tramps dance with Judy Garland in *Easter Parade*, Astaire isn't all that great when he goes downmarket to do raucous comedy. The other memorable dance in the movie is that in which, when his sister is late for a rehearsal while aboard an ocean liner bound for England, Astaire's Tom Bowen character improvises a charming dance with a clothes tree. Perhaps at this point it begins to seem as if that clothes tree, with one notable exception, was Fred Astaire's best partner.

Apart from Ginger Rogers, Astaire never made more than two movies with the same partner. With a now-forgotten actress named Lucille Bremer he made one and (roughly) one twentieth of a movie. He danced two big numbers with her in *Ziegfeld Follies* in 1946—one in Chinese costume and the other to Harry Warren's song "This Heart of Mine," in which Miss Bremer wears a white gown and he is in white tie and tails with red sash. They did a large movie, an extravaganza really, the same year called *Yolanda and the Thief*, which tells the old story of a con man who, his swindle accomplished, gets a conscience. Astaire plays the con man Johnny Parkson Riggs, Miss Bremer his immensely wealthy mark Yolanda, with supporting roles played by Frank Morgan and Mildred Natwick. The movie was a commercial flop, though the acute John Mueller calls it, for reasons not entirely clear to me, "an interesting failure."

Part of the blame for the failure, all who were in on it aver, goes to Vincente Minnelli, the director, with whom Astaire wanted to work, but who apparently cut the film drastically and by doing so made it much worse. Part goes, too, to the always disappointing fact that Astaire is not permitted to dance enough; he does only two dances and sings one song in the movie. A further part of the failure is owing to Ms. Bremer, who, after this movie, was given no further starring movie roles and by 1948 disappeared from the movies to marry the wealthy son of a former president of Mexico, which was probably the right career move. She was not much smaller than Fred Astaire but seemed to have wider shoulders. Her emotional range as an actress was narrow, her range as a dancer no wider.

Lucille Bremer did only heavy-breathing drama. In *Yolanda and the Thief*, she does a very long balletic dance (lasting for sixteen minutes) that is supposed to be taking place in Johnny's troubled sleep. The dance itself has an overdramatized pretentiousness of a kind that one associates with Gene Kelly at his worst. The other dance number in the movie comes toward its end, taking place at a carnival, where Astaire and Bremer do a fine energetic jitterbuggy Spanish dance on a swirly black-and-white marble floor. The number has a bit of lead-in dialogue of unconscious comedy, when Yolanda says to Johnny, "Let's go and watch the dancing." *Watch the dancing!* In an Astaire movie, the line is equivalent to "Do you think she'll be ready for the Derby, gramps?"

Things look up—way up—with *Easter Parade*, the only movie co-starring Fred Astaire and Judy Garland. In good measure this is owed to Miss Garland, who of course had camera magic. Once a camera was running, she could make herself seem enormously appealing in a vast range of moods and manners. Astaire has this same magic, though with much less emotional range; but if his emotional range is more restricted than Miss Garland's, this movie allows him to exhibit his full range as a dancer: from novelty to comedy to pop to romantic dancing. Although Judy Garland was twenty-five when the movie was made and Astaire forty-eight, the difference in their ages doesn't seem to signify.

Astaire's part in the movie was originally intended for Gene Kelly, who broke his ankle and (it will be recalled) suggested Astaire for the part. The second female romantic lead, though originally to be played by Cyd Charisse, is instead Ann Miller. All the dances were designed for Kelly, but Astaire reshaped them to fit his own lighter, more dashing style. Vincente Minnelli was supposed to direct, but owing to his by-then-troubled marriage to Miss Garland, stepped down to make way for Charles Walters, himself a former dancer and choreographer.

The story line, briefly, is that Don Hewes (Astaire) is in love with Nadine Hale (Miller), a former dance partner who rejects him when better professional opportunities turn up, so he decides to make good his claim to her that he doesn't really need her and that he can train anyone to do what she did. And so in a bar he picks out Hannah Brown (Garland), who is working in a chorus line, to be his new partner. Peter Lawford plays Jonathan Harrow III, the loyal friend in love with Hannah, who realizes that she loves Don more. Don will eventually discover what a sweet character Hannah is and fall in love with her. End film to strains of the song "Easter Parade."

Lots of things make this movie successful, not least among them no fewer than seventeen songs by Irving Berlin, including, of course, the title song. (Why is it that Jewish songwriters composed all the popular songs for Christian holidays? How come Cole Porter never wrote a song for Rosh Hashanah or Noël Coward one for Purim? A question to be sent on to the Anti-Defamation League, perhaps.) Astaire's clothes in this movie are especially knockout. No one ever wore a top hat more jauntily than

he, and the angle at which he wore it was never more rak-
ish than in this movie.

But the key element behind the pleasure that *Easter Parade* gives is that there is a lot more singing and dancing in
it than in any other Astaire movie. Clearly, the recipe for
a successful Fred Astaire movie is the least possible plot,
or at any rate the least time devoted to working out the
plot, leaving more time for singing and dancing. This
movie is the musical comedy equivalent of contemporary
action movies in which something—a car chase, a leap
from a cliff, an escape from a burning building—is supposed to happen every eighty seconds (I may have the
exact time between violent actions wrong, but you get the
point). So in *Easter Parade*, very little time is allowed to
pass between song-and-dance numbers, and this is all for
the best.

The most memorable number in *Easter Parade*—I remembered it some fifty years after seeing the movie when
it was first shown—is "We're a Couple of Swells." In this
number, Astaire and Garland, got up in tramp clothes,
each with a front tooth blackened out, dance and sing
about their being somewhat discommoded at arriving at
Mrs. Vanderbilt's tea party, to which they, as a "couple of
swells," have been invited. Everything here works to the
highest power. This is also the only dance in all his thirty-

three movie-musical roles in which Fred Astaire may have been outshone by a partner; next to Judy Garland, he seems, for the first and only time, not quite the main attraction.

Although Miss Garland was originally daunted by Astaire, his star status, and his reputation as a man driven by perfectionism, the two ended up holding each other, quite properly, in the highest regard as fellow professionals. As mentioned earlier, she was slated to make two further movies with Fred Astaire: *The Barkleys of Broadway* and *Royal Wedding*, but was unable to do either. As a great showman himself, Astaire was fully aware of Miss Garland's own immense showmanship, and he later claimed that working with her was a piece of great good luck and one of the best things to happen to his career. Had Garland and Astaire gone on to make these other movies, their impress as a team might have been stronger on the American consciousness, and the Fred and Ginger duo might have been eclipsed somewhat by the Judy and Fred duo (in *Easter Parade*, Garland received billing above Astaire).

Fred Astaire and Audrey Hepburn as co-stars of *Funny Face* sounds as if it ought to have been a perfect pairing. She was eager to appear in a movie with him, and he, in response to speculation whether it was possible to "get him" for a movie with her, replied: "What do you mean *if* you can get me? I'm already excited. Audrey Hepburn? That's the dream of my life!" Astaire and Hepburn, each on his or her own, represented the moviegoer's ultimate notion of high style.

The two were similar in being bone thin and wearing clothes wonderfully well. Astaire's accent was mid-Atlantic, and Hepburn's was English. Her general look was that of the gamine, or boy-girl, delicate, refined, un-zaftig, which was very much Astaire's ideal type. The movie critic David Thomson wrote of Audrey Hepburn that "she seemed English; she had a sense of manners and kindness that came close to grace; and she achieved a 'look'—the knockout *gamin* who inspired a generation of thin, flat-chested, upper-class girls." She also gave off the aura of having good character, which, witness her serious charitable works late in her relatively short life (she died of cancer at sixty-three), she apparently really did have.

Audrey Hepburn, who was born in 1929, played opposite a number of much older men: Humphrey Bogart, Gregory Peck, William Holden, Cary Grant, Gary Cooper. But until now, in *Funny Face*, she wasn't asked to dance with one of them. Dancing with a man, romantically dancing with him, because it is so physically intimate, is much different from exchanging witticisms with an older man, in the approved mode of romantic comedy. Fred Astaire was fifty-eight when he made *Funny Face*, Audrey Hepburn was twenty-eight. The question was, Could he keep up with her off the dance floor without looking either tired or randy? Then, too, because Astaire was Astaire, and hence an extraordinary physical phenomenon, could Audrey Hepburn keep up with him on the dance floor?

Somehow Astaire was able to bring off being the lover of a woman thirty years younger than he without seeming an old lech. But Audrey Hepburn, though she was said to have had some training in ballet, wasn't really able to keep up as a dancer with Fred Astaire. They dance together three times in the movie. Once in a darkroom, with a backdrop of red lighting; the other two times with Ms. Hepburn wearing a wedding dress for a photo shoot for the fashion magazine for which they both work, she as a model, he as a Richard Avedon–like star photographer. In all three dances Astaire is firmly at the helm. Hepburn does not embarrass herself—as she comes close to doing in a sad solo that is a satire of modern dance called "Basal Metabolism." But apart from Hepburn's lovely face, with its high cheekbones and large lush brown eyes, Astaire could really have been dancing with a thousand other women. Physically, spiritually, Hepburn, had she been twenty years older or he twenty years younger, might have been Fred Astaire's ideal partner, with one insurmountable proviso: she didn't have the nerves and muscles of a true dancer.

Much of this is covered over by the lavishness of *Funny Face*, many of whose sets were designed by Richard Avedon—designed, in one notable montage, to look like a spread in *Vogue*, whose most famous photographer Avedon was at the time. Other scenes, including one in which Astaire and Miss Hepburn dance, she in a wedding dress, are shot with a soft-focus lens, which gives the misty quality once used in the old Kotex magazine ads. All this was thought artistic in its day; now it all feels a bit heavy-handed: edgy today becomes corny tomorrow. Astaire deserves a special award for appearing in a great many scenes in this movie with a camera hanging around his neck—never, a camera, a swank piece of jewelry—and yet lugging this camera around neither daunts him nor detracts from his own easy elegance.

In *Funny Face*, Astaire also does, with the actress Kay Thompson, a parody of an Elvis-like rock 'n' roller, in which he wears a goatee and mustache and totes a guitar. The number is very strenuous—he seems to spend lots of time on the floor—but doesn't come off, and suggests that while Astaire could do comedy dancing as well as almost anybody (Donald O'Connor and Ray Bolger perhaps excepted), it is not for comedy that we look to him but for romance and grace and suavity. Kay Thompson, according to the screenwriter Leonard Gershe, was "the only dancing partner he didn't cotton to," finding her too strong, almost masculine in her approach to dance.

Bing Crosby was not, in the strict sense, a dancing partner of Fred Astaire's, but Astaire made two movies with him in which they danced together: *Holiday Inn* and *Blue Skies*. Even though each man held the other in great esteem, the partnership only half worked. In *Blue Skies*, they danced and sang to "A Couple of Song and Dance Men," which of course is what they were, with Crosby as the song, and no need to add who was the dance, man. The number is comic, remembering that the difference between "comic" and "comical" is that the first word speaks to intention, the second to effect. The humor between the two men doesn't often work in either picture. Crosby and Astaire never succeeded in the way that Crosby and Hope, in their *Road* movies, did; the rivalrousness and put-downs didn't really take.

In both the Crosby-Astaire movies, Crosby gets the girl, which puts Astaire in the position of being irritatingly on the make, and hence both a bit of a hustler and more than a bit of a loser. He is, to be sure, a good loser, but a loser nonetheless. We should never feel sorry for Fred Astaire; we should instead be rooting for him, dazzled by him, delighted at his gentle conquest of the girl. Which may partly explain why these movies don't succeed. Besides, why would any sensible woman choose the not very graceful, crooning Crosby, with his shapeless body and less than subtle face, over Fred Astaire? It makes no sense.

The plots do not help clear things up. In *Holiday Inn*, Jim Hardy (Crosby) breaks up his old show-biz team to start a country hotel that will be open only on certain holidays, for each of which he prepares a show. (This is the movie in which Crosby introduced Irving Berlin's "White Christmas.") He is followed in this endeavor by Linda Mason, played by the actress Marjorie Reynolds, whom Ted Hanover (Astaire) ardently pursues. She eventually goes for Jim, for reasons only God or Paramount Studio can explain. In *Blue Skies*, Astaire's Jed Potter loses out on Joan Caulfield, whose character, Mary O'Hara, is mad for Crosby's Johnny Adams. Johnny has this odd little tic of opening extravagant night clubs and then, once they appear to be succeeding, selling them off and moving on, which makes his being a husband and father to a blondish too-cute-to-be-believed child very difficult. Astaire's role is to wait in the wings, matrimonially speaking, for Mary to give up on Johnny and marry him. She never does.

But his movies with Bing Crosby do provide Astaire the opportunity to do two memorable solo dances: "Let's Say It with Firecrackers" in *Holiday Inn*, in which he punctuates an energetic Fourth of July tap dance with a magnificent crescendo-building tossing of firecrackers on the floor before him while wearing a star-spangled ascot, socks, and bandana around his waist. In *Blue Skies*, he does a reprise of sorts on his great "Top Hat, White Tie, and Tails" dance, this time around to another Irving Berlin song, "Puttin' on the Ritz," with a chorus of dancers composed of six reproduced versions of himself, with other novelties added, such as slow-motion camera work and a wonderful bit of business with a cane. Astaire, who handled objects so adeptly, would have made a splendid juggler.

The youngest dancer Fred Astaire was paired with after Joan Leslie was the French actress Leslie Caron, who, despite a fair amount of balletic training, never seemed quite comfortable dancing with Astaire. Astaire's role in *Daddy Long Legs*, the movie they did together, was as the secret benefactor of the orphaned Miss Caron, which nicely took care of the thirty-two-year difference in their ages. She is too chunky for the sleek Astaire, and too klunky for the smooth Astaire: "stiff, unyielding, uncomprehending" is the way John Mueller, accurately, describes her performance in this movie. Astaire does one of his drum dances in the movie—he does another in *The Belle of New York*—and a fine little business gliding off on a tea cart in a hotel corridor. Johnny Mercer's song "Something's Gotta Give" is tailor-made for Astairish dancing. Yet even this lilting song can't limber up poor Miss Caron. She seemed nowhere near so awkward dancing with Gene Kelly in *An American in Paris*. But it may well have been that as a dancer she was more adept at the dramatic than at the sophisticated: she also dances in a nightmare ballet in *Daddy Long Legs* that doesn't help move the movie along. Fred Astaire was able to elevate the talents of many of the women he danced with, but in the case of Leslie Caron, things never quite got off the ground.

Astaire did two movies with Cyd Charisse, *The Band Wagon* and *Silk Stockings*. *The Band Wagon* is another version of the old "Hey-kids-whaddya-say-we-put-on-a-show?" story. Some have read this movie to be a story about Astaire's own life—that of a movie star who has lost his luster and tries to regain it by returning to the stage—

but if this was the movie's intention, its ineptitude as a roman à clef is impressive: Fred Astaire never came close to being washed up. His various announced retirements were all at his own discretion. *Silk Stockings* is the movie version of a Melchior Lengyel play called *Ninotchka*, originally made into a nonmusicial film by Ernst Lubitsch and starring Greta Garbo. For its *Silk Stockings* adaptation Cole Porter wrote the music.

Along with Rita Hayworth and Ava Gardner, Cyd Charisse was one of the most beautiful women ever to appear in movies. Like Hayworth and Gardner, her beauty was of the smoldering sexy kind, in her case overlaid with a patina of unapproachable chill; she had sublime legs and a rather immobile face, detached and distant, with perfect features that somehow suggested depth (a suggestion completely wiped out by her choosing to marry the singer Tony Martin, a man whose vanity far exceeds his talent). Her entrance to show business was through her good looks and her dancing; her training was in ballet. At 5-foot-6 and 112 pounds, she came close to being too large for Astaire. Playing on this fact, in *The Band Wagon* there is a brief scene, a little joke, in which Astaire sidles up to her to make sure that he is taller than she.

Cyd Charisse's dancing, as befits a ballerina, tended to be dramatic rather than witty, so the best dances she and

Astaire did together were romantic ones: to "Dancing in the Dark" in *The Band Wagon*, to "All of You" in *Silk Stockings*. In *The Band Wagon*, they attempted a dance of heightened drama called "Girl Hunt Ballet"—a parody, in dance, of a Mickey Spillane novel—which feels as if it were choreographed for Gene Kelly and which doesn't work, though it took seven days and cost more than $300,000 to film, a big figure at that time. Of it John Mueller writes: "This duet is notable for its strained efforts at hardsell, its ersatz sexiness, and its lack of musical wit and sophistication—qualities which strongly suggest that Astaire had little to do with its choreography," which was in fact done by a man named Michael Kidd.

What disqualified Cyd Charisse as a perfect partner for Fred Astaire was a want of lightheartedness, of sauciness, of wit. She could move but she couldn't groove. She was too dramatic, too earnest, too sexy, even too beautiful to meet the job's requirements.

Barrie Chase was Fred Astaire's final dance partner, not in the movies but on television. (She appeared in a bit part in *Silk Stockings*.) They did four television specials together between the years 1959 and 1968: *An Evening with Fred Astaire*, *Another Evening with Fred Astaire*, *Astaire Time*, and *The Fred Astaire Show*, when Astaire was sixty-nine; all won critical appreciation, high ratings, Emmys, the works. Barrie Chase was twenty-two, Astaire fifty-nine when they did their first show together. (Astaire never put on weight; the color of his sleek wigs remained the same till his seventies, when he ordered them with gray trimmings; he covered his doubtless sagging neck with bright ties and ascots and bandanas; the only place he showed his age was in what seemed to be the wrinkling of his skin and the lengthening of his chin.) Chase was small enough to wear high heels when dancing with him, very beautiful in his preferred gamine mode, with what used to be called a fine figure (now known as a great bod). She could do tap and ballroom, staccato rhythm and rolling fluidity, with equal aplomb.

The vast difference in their ages put Astaire beyond the dirty-old-man image that had come more and more to worry him. Barrie Chase was au courant in dress and spirit, with marvelous haircuts, stylish in the best feminine way. They were swell together, and watching them one thinks what a pity she wasn't older or he much younger, so that their knockout dancing didn't have the slight touch of freakishness about it that his age lent to the proceedings. Hermes Pan, Astaire's co-choreographer in many of his movies, said Astaire "liked Barrie Chase's dancing very much. He thought she was a beautiful mover." Stanley Donen said that Barrie Chase was the woman with whom Fred Astaire most enjoyed dancing, and there were even rumors about his having a romantic interest in her.

Almost all the women who danced with Fred Astaire were daunted by him. He represented an ideal; he expected them to put in long rehearsal time. Much talk of women going off in tears. (On the other side, Debbie Reynolds, then nineteen years old and in a movie with Gene Kelly, felt utterly defeated by the demands Kelly made upon her, when Astaire came by, helped her with her routine, and put her back in the game with restored high spirits.) He wasn't cruel; merely demanding in an authoritative way. "How do you think those routines were accomplished," Ginger Rogers said in an interview in *Family Circle*. "With mirrors? Well, I thought I knew what concentrated work was before I met Fred, but he's the limit. Never satisfied until every detail is right, and he will not compromise. No sir! What's more, if he thinks of something better after you've finished a routine, you do it over."

Astaire was too much the gent ever to say, at least in public, that one or another of his partners was inadequate in any way. When asked, he told people he was lucky to have danced with lots of beautiful women. But most of these women knew very well that, in the end, the privilege was theirs. "I guess the only jewels of my life," said Rita Hayworth, "were the pictures I made with Fred Astaire."

Must You Dance, Every Dance

Which brings us back to Ginger Rogers. Why should this actress, a Hollywood type not far off the standard, with no special training as a dancer, have been the best of all Fred Astaire's partners, in many ways the making of his film career and perhaps the chief guarantor of his place in the history of entertainment and, many would say, of terpsichorean art?

In the reality of Hollywood, all of Astaire's objections to being teamed with Ginger Rogers were finally beside the point. The television sports producer Don Ohlmeyer, when approached by a young reporter saying that he had a question for him, replied, "If the question is about sports, the answer is money." The same applies, redoubled, to the movies. The RKO producer Pandro S. Berman, in response to Astaire's protestations about continuing his partnership with Ginger Rogers, wired Astaire's agent: "Ginger Rogers seems to go rather well with him and there is no need to assume we will be making permanent team of this pair except if we can all clean up a lot of money by keeping them together would be foolish not to." And only until they ceased to clean up a lot of money—about six films further—was anything like serious thought given to breaking up the Astaire and Rogers team.

Of the partnership, Arlene Croce writes that Ginger Rogers "brought out his toughness and also his true masculine gallantry." She could also act while dancing; only with her did there seem to be genuine emotions passing between partners while on the dance floor. "Rogers was outstanding among Astaire's film partners not because she was superior to the others as a dancer but because, as a skilled, intuitive actress, she was cagey enough to realize that acting did not stop where dancing began," wrote John Mueller. "She seemed uniquely to understand the dramatic import of the dance, and, without resorting to style-shattering emoting, she cunningly contributed her share to the choreographic impact of their numbers together. The point of many of these was joy; indeed, the reason so many women have fantasized about dancing with Fred Astaire is that Ginger Rogers conveyed the impression that dancing with him is the most thrilling experience imaginable."

Sheilah Graham, the Hollywood columnist and great good friend of F. Scott Fitzgerald, who knew Astaire fairly well, wrote: "He danced later with other girls who were better dancers than Ginger, like Cyd Charisse and Eleanor Powell and Rita Hayworth, but none of them came off like Ginger came off. She was a beautiful doll who looked innocent and very happy. The combination was terrific. Fred was never as good with anyone else." Or, as Arlene Croce, apropos of Astaire without Rogers, wrote: "It was a world of sun without a moon."

Despite all the talk of Fred Astaire bringing "class" to the partnership, it might be closer to the truth to say that it was Ginger Rogers who brought class—specifically, something of the lower middle or maybe even the working class. In pursuing Ginger Rogers in the movies they did together, Astaire may have been going a bit downmarket, in the way that Charles Swann goes after Odette de Crecy, the cocotte of Marcel Proust's great novel. Not that the Ginger Rogers roles resembled in the faintest the character of Odette in Proustian complexity, but there is a common masculine fantasy about the pleasures promised by girls of a lower class than one's own: the fantasy being that they are more passionate, somehow wilder than those of one's own class; there is the accompanying fantasy that one can bring such a girl up to one's level and show her, as they say, the finer things. There is, of course, nothing to any of this, as poor Charles Swann learns to his chagrin, but the presence of hard evidence rarely kills a fantasy.

Conversely, many girls from the middle classes and below must think that life spent with a man of the upper classes, which Astaire seemed to represent (even though Astaire's own origins in Omaha, Nebraska, as we have seen, were far from upper class), was the highway to heaven. Ginger Rogers could play feisty, perky, sassy, cute, ticked-off, sensitive, vulnerable, but there was also a vulgar streak to her—and this touch of vulgarity, when she was young, could translate as sexy. When she grew older, heavier, used thick makeup—as a Christian Scientist, she never had the option of cosmetic surgery—the sexy faded away, leaving the vulgarity to dominate.

The young Ginger Rogers was the perfect size for Astaire: perhaps 5-foot-3 or 5-foot-4, she weighed 105 pounds, which made it easier for him to execute tosses and lifts with her. She seemed to fit into his arms more snugly, more perfectly, than any of his other partners. She could look marvelously slender in slacks, which she often wore for their dance numbers, yet pleasingly fleshy in gowns. She had the perfect dancer's body—perfect, specifically, for the combination of ballroom and tap dancing that was Astaire's specialty. She didn't tote around a big bosom, she had good legs, a lovely back, a slenderness that seemed pliant, sensual, never bordering on the skinny.

She was also twelve years younger then he, in some ways the perfect age separation, making him seem more the man of the world, her the young woman coming into full bloom. A reviewer in the *New York Herald-Tribune* wrote that *The Gay Divorcee*, their first movie together as stars, "gives the freshly charming Miss Rogers an opportunity to prove she's almost as perfect an example of feminine desirability in musical comedy as Myrna Loy is in drama." This doesn't feel quite right. Myrna Loy was more reserved, more naturally refined, hence somehow more sexually concealed than Ginger Rogers, who was more in the mode of a what-you-see-is-what-you-get kind of girl. But what you were likely to get wasn't bad at all; it was pretty damn fine, in fact.

Sexy outside of steamy—sexy as fun, not heavy-breathing, bouncy but not sweaty—this is what the young Ginger Rogers conveyed. Such kittenish sexiness, with a strong aroma of the witty behind it, is what Fred Astaire needed to play against to show himself to greatest advantage. Not for him to push a grapefruit into a complaining woman's face, or to ask why "of all the gin joints in all the towns in all the world, she walks into mine"— this kind of thing, as mentioned earlier, wasn't available to Astaire. Although when required he could sing and dance to "Night and Day" (the beat, beat, beat of those damn tom-toms) and went in for a bit of "Dancing in the Dark," he did best dancing as energetic, joyous, honest delight. Ginger, as the name suggests, provided the perfect seasoning.

That Ginger Rogers was not a professional dancer, with long experience in ballet or tap, was probably an added benefit. What it meant, in practice, was that Fred Astaire, through relentless rehearsal, in effect trained her—and trained her above all to dance his way and with him. In a great many stills of the two dancing, one notes Astaire's large hand around Rogers's waist, rather like a short but firm leash, always in place lest she wander too far away. Ann Richards's feminist joke that Ginger Rogers did everything Fred Astaire did except backward and in high heels doesn't quite hold up, for without his instruction she might never have been able to do it anywhere near so well forward, even in Michael Jordan Nike Airs.

A good measure of the success behind the Astaire-Rogers partnership is also owed to the fact that they came together at a time when an extraordinary clutch of great songwriters was at work—many of them at the peak of their powers. Jerome Kern, Cole Porter, the Gershwins, and, above all for Astaire and Rogers, Irving Berlin were, as the psychobabblists have it, there for them. Most of these songwriters took pleasure in writing for Astaire, and George Gershwin and Irving Berlin came to be his good friends.

No one has ever been able to explain the clustering of talent that shows up at certain points in history: the genius composers who arrived in Austria and Germany in the eighteenth century, the great Russian fiction writers in the middle to late nineteenth century, the brilliant German physicists in the early decades of the twentieth century. At a doubtless lower level of significance, the men and women who wrote for—who really created—musical comedy through the medium of the jazz song provide another example of the phenomenon of talent appearing in clusters, then, *bang!*, pretty much vanishing forever.

Without this impressive songwriting talent supporting him, Fred Astaire might never have achieved what he did. He for his part greatly promoted these songwriters by giving their work the widest possible hearing in his movies. (Astaire himself is mentioned by name in a number of their songs, the most famous such reference being Cole Porter's, from "You're The Top": "You're the nimble tread of the feet of Fred Astaire," with Astaire rhymed in the next line with Camembert.) But it was not his voice alone but the rhythms he felt in his body that meshed so beautifully with the work of these songwriters. *Symbiosis* is probably too strong a word to describe the relationship between Astaire and the songwriters of the era, yet Irving Berlin said, "I never would have written 'Top Hat, White Tie, and Tails,' or 'Cheek to Cheek,' or 'Isn't This a Lovely Day' if I didn't have Astaire and Rogers to write to." Astaire said: "I just loved his music and I was delighted when they got him to do this [the score for *Top Hat*]. And Irving thought the same about getting me to do it because he liked the way I did things." That's not immodest; it's just true.

The Fred Astaire and Ginger Rogers partnership was not the work of careful calculation by the movie geniuses. She just happened to be available when his early pictures were about to be made. For their first lead roles together, in *The Gay Divorcee*, Astaire didn't want Ginger Rogers, thinking a woman with an English accent better suited to the part. Critics of intellectual standing who reviewed their early films—James Agate, Alistair Cooke, Graham

Greene—also missed the magic residing in this pairing. Only moviegoers seemed to understand that something out of the ordinary was going on. *The Gay Divorcee* was a great hit at the box office. The young Pandro S. Berman saw that the Astaire-Rogers coupling was the white donkey upon which he and RKO could ride into Jerusalem. Like Astaire, Berman soon acquired a ten percent share in the gross of these movies, and so perhaps rode into Jerusalem instead in a Rolls-Royce.

Berman lined up movie after movie for the two—well, actually, seven of the ten movies they did together—and he brought in the right supporting comic actors to act as their foils: Edward Everett Horton, Eric Blore, Erik Rhodes, Helen Broderick, Victor Moore, Franklin Pangborn, Alice Brady, and others. A word needs to be said on behalf of the great skill of these supporting actors and for the dab hand of the casting directors who chose them. They were the ones who kept the flimsy plots of the Astaire-Rogers movies afloat. Their comic talents brought buoyancy, wit, frothy silliness, frivolous charm to roles of no more than comic-book complexity.

The Art Nouveau sets of plush hotel suites and lush lobbies and staterooms on luxury liners, in pellucid black and white done by Van Nest Polglase, provided the perfect background for the smart life that the most of the characters in these movies are supposed to represent. They also gave moviegoers a glimpse of the fantasy of high life during the dreary days of the Depression. Although Astaire longed to work in Technicolor, black and white seemed to bring out the glittering best in his talent. (Something there is inherently glamorous about the combination of black and white, tuxedo colors and the colors, too, of Truman Capote's great celebrity party for 540 of his closest friends at the Plaza Hotel in 1966.) "That Black and White Baby of Mine" is the title of a Cole Porter song of the day; someone, glomming on to the glamour residing in the combination, named a once popular scotch whisky Black & White.

Arlene Croce felt that Astaire and Rogers first really clicked artistically as a team in *Roberta*, their third movie together, when, in rehearsal clothes, they do their first zowie dance number together to "I'll Be Hard to Handle." That number, she writes,

> is the big event of the film, the number in which
> "Fred and Ginger" became fixed screen deities.
> The wonderful secret they seemed to share in
> "The Continental" [the big final number in *The
> Gay Divorcee*] becomes here a magical rapport that
> is sustained through three minutes of what looks

like sheerest improvisation. It begins with some light banter punctuated by dance breaks, continues with music and more dance breaks—a tap conversation with each taking eight-bar "sentences" (his growing more impudent, hers more indignant)— and ends in a chain of turns across the floor and a flop into two chairs.

This was the dance, according to Miss Croce, that marked the occasion when Astaire and Rogers had effectively worked out genuine screen personalities against which each could play off the other, for wit, laughs, conflict, romance. Hard enough though it is to create an individual style, what the two together had succeeded in doing was developing differing styles that somehow blended into a duet, or couple, style—one that would never be equaled in the history of dancing, in the movies or anywhere else.

Benny Green makes the useful point that Fred Astaire and Ginger Rogers freed dancing in the movies from the geometrical straitjacket that the choreographer-director Busby Berkeley had imposed upon it. Berkeley's taste ran to the big production number, scores of uniformly costumed girls doing kicks or marching steps in unison, photographed from above—the equivalent of synchronized swimming, or the Radio City Rockettes, a Rose Bowl game shot from the Goodyear blimp. The jazz critic Stanley Crouch, who compares Astaire's innovation in dancing on film to Louis Armstrong's great solo style in jazz, writes that

> Astaire had no need for a logistical visual genius like Busby Berkeley. Astaire wanted the camera to serve the dancer so that all the complexity, nuance, and expression would be the dancer's responsibility. He would not stand for crosscutting or anything other than the camera being far enough away to capture his entire body. The reason: His instrument [as a dancer] stretched from the top of his head to the bottom of his feet. Novelty shots and startling setups were replaced with a luminescent individual power held in place by an overwhelming ease. Astaire gave the impression that the way he was moving at any moment was three things plaited together: the only, the most natural, and the *best* choice.

Edwin Denby, who thought a good bit about the resources of film for capturing dance—and ballet and modern dance are never caught anywhere near so well on film as in person, where the eye can travel wherever it wishes—thought dancing on film best when shot at the close middle distance and when the dancing itself is not highly dramatized. "A dance style like Astaire's," Denby wrote,

which makes a fine art of understatement, is for this reason the immediately effective style in a film. It looks natural a few feet away. It does so not merely for the psychological reason that tap dancing is what we think of as a natural way of dancing in this country, but much more because tap dancing lends itself technically to an exquisite salon style. The dynamic range is narrow but sharply differentiated; the dramatic miming is barely indicated but perfectly intelligible; the presentation is intimately charming; and the dance itself rarely needs much room. A complete dance phrase can generally be photographed close by in a single camera field, and the continuity to the following phrase is generally so casual that a shift in the camera between phrases does not interrupt very much. These are the technical advantages which allow Astaire—who is certainly a great dancer—to give a more complete sense of dance expression on the screen than good dancers in other styles can.

Astaire himself may not have been able to formulate this same point with the same nicety, but he instinctively understood and acted on it.

Few people are alive today who can report on Astaire's stage dancing. Merce Cunningham, the modern dance choreographer, has said, "I'm not sorry that I saw him only on film." I take him to mean that Astaire was at his best caught on camera. In an interview with Anna Kisselgoff, then the *New York Times*' chief dance critic, Cunningham took particular pleasure in Astaire's "wit and play with steps, going slightly ahead of the beat and again delaying to stretch something a fraction . . . the sheer pleasure of his dancing—a quality that makes us lose track of mental gymnastics. It gives the mind a rest and the spirit a big boost."

When Astaire and Rogers danced on film, all was fluid, smooth, free-flowing. No one could imagine much enjoyment from dancing in a Busby Berkeley number, but lots of people could fantasize themselves as Fred Astaire and Ginger Rogers. When an audience watched Astaire and Rogers, Benny Green writes, "it was dreaming of its own existence. . . . This sense of identity was to have astonishing effects on the dance-hall business in the 1930s. Every man wanted to woo every lady by dancing at, with, or round her. Astaire and Rogers had succeeded in resolving the complexities of an arcane and physically demanding exercise into a truly democratic pastime." (Astaire, under his wife's guidance, began a large number of Fred Astaire Dance Studios in 1947, but they didn't do well; meanwhile, a man named Arthur Murray, nowhere near the dancer Astaire was, cleaned up with his dance studios. The Fred Astaire Studios have since been revived, though under different ownership.)

Alexis de Tocqueville would doubtless have had fascinating things to say about the mixed democratic-aristocratic element in the Astaire-Rogers team. In a number of their movies together, the fools (nicely played by Erik Rhodes and Eric Blore, among others) are inevitably European, some ostensibly aristocratic. But the only true aristocrat was, of course, Fred Astaire—an aristocrat of talent. Tocqueville understood that nowhere was aristocratic style more admired than in a democracy, and so, too, one must suppose, deep in his canny producer's heart did Pandro S. Berman know this.

As for Ginger Rogers, in her movies with Astaire she played a woman alone, usually struggling to keep her own fragile craft afloat in the stormy seas of big-city life. Often she is in circumstances—working as a dance instructor, pretending to be a countess in Paris, trying to get into show biz—in which she can go under at any time.

She's the gutsy girl, the tough kid, spunky, yet at the same time delicate, vulnerable, so readily imagined as defeated that she must be saved. This, too, is a democratic archetype—the sweet girl making her way in an unforgiving big-city environment; much earlier this same type was captured by Theodore Dreiser in *Sister Carrie*.

The notion of a democratic aristocracy, in which everything came easily—everyone living in the glint of glamour (those lovely black-and-white Van Nest Polglase backgrounds), with no conflict more complex than how do we get these sweet goofy kids, Fred and Ginger, together—had a special appeal in the dour years of the 1930s. (The Astaire-Rogers movies ran from *Flying Down to Rio* in 1933 to *The Story of Vernon and Irene Castle* in 1939, with *The Barkleys of Broadway* coming as an afterthought in 1949.) The timing, in other words, was right for the Astaire-Rogers partnership: talking movies were still young enough to attempt interesting changes, a lustrous cadre of songwriters was on the scene, and an audience whose lives were greatly stinted by economic depression was ready to entertain—more important, to be entertained by—the fantasy of easy elegance.

And there was something distinctly fantastical about the coupling of Fred Astaire, a man who looked like no other but still looked great, and Ginger Rogers, the blonde of blondes (her true hair color was brown), the babe (but no bimbo) of babes, dancing their way through everyone else's hard times. If the Hollywood of those days was a dream machine, it never constructed a better dream than that of these two actors, a skinny likable guy who could move like no one else in the world and a dish who, though not a professional dancer, was in her own way a classic American type. Arlene Croce describes Ginger Rogers's dancing as "refreshingly laconic. It was dancing at its driest and shapeliest; it had none of the excesses, nothing of the sweet tooth of its period. And though half the time in the slow duets we're contemplating the beauty of her body, we can see that it's also an expressive body—that the back is strong and whiplike as well as beautifully molded, the waist long and sinuous, the hips free, the chest open. Feet and hands are delicious."

Were they, Astaire and Rogers, also sexy as a couple? Miss Croce writes of their "exquisite sexual harmony that made them not only the ideal dancing couple but the ideal romantic team." I myself think they were more glamorous than sexy. And yet they were glamorous, too, in a democratic way: with some strain, nearly every man or woman could imagine him- or herself being like Astaire or like Rogers. They were glamorous, in other words, without losing the common touch. Miss Croce calls them "the two most divinely *usual* people in the history of movies." That word *usual* connotes the democratic element.

Sex isn't primarily what the partnership was about. One imagines sexy people at, well, sex, in bed, going at it, bonking away, two-backed beast, and all that. One rarely imagines Astaire and Rogers thus. In fact, until their final three movies together (*Carefree, The Story of Vernon and Irene Castle,* and *The Barkleys of Broadway,* in the latter two of which they play a married couple), they were notable for not even kissing, which was probably a good idea. One doesn't want to think of this elegant pair actually making love, certainly nowhere near a camera. No pressing need, really, for such a couple to dance between the sheets when they danced so wondrously outside them.

With all this going for them, why did the Astaire-Rogers team break up? The subsidiary reasons are several. One, as we have seen, is that each thought he or she could do better without the other. Another is the absence of even passable screenplays that could maintain their momentum as a movie team. But the chief reason—

always the chief reason in Hollywood—once again is money. RKO, the studio at which Astaire and Rogers made their great splash, fell back into serious financial trouble. The Astaire-Rogers team was slipping in popularity. Their movies all made money, but after a while less and less money. Soon they dropped out of the top ten movie attractions. In the end, the two were allowed to separate only when the money went elsewhere.

Astaire and Rogers tried it again, one last time, for MGM, in *The Barkleys of Broadway*. But it was no good; it was over. Ginger Rogers took on the movie because her own career was slumping; she was thirty-eight in 1948 when it was made. She had thickened, especially around the upper back, shoulders, and arms. (She recites the "Marseillaise" in the movie in a rendition so wretched it could have stopped the French Revolution.) Astaire remained the same lean, clean dancing machine, but in Ginger Rogers he was now assigned to partner a somewhat matronly woman, like your batty Aunt Lurlene who was always slightly embarrassing dancing at other people's weddings. This was not a good idea, never what the Astaire-Rogers team was about: it was always about youth, especially beautiful female youth. They had had their time—roughly five brilliant years, from 1933 to

1938—and it couldn't be recaptured. Over, done, kaput, yet seventy years later still marvelous to revisit. Watching them together at their best, Astaire and Rogers, Fred and Ginger, still makes one want get out on the dance floor and give it one's own best (of course, next to them, comparatively pathetic) shot.

And I Trust, You'll Excuse My Dust

In *A Mathematician's Apology*, the Cambridge don G. H. Hardy, justifying his life as a mathematician, writes: "It is a tiny minority who can do anything really well, and the number of men [today we should of course add 'and women'] who can do two things well is negligible." Underscoring Hardy's last point, Oscar Levant, in his day the wittiest man in Hollywood, informed of Marilyn Monroe's decision to divorce Joe DiMaggio, is said to have remarked: "I guess no one can expect to excel at more than one national pastime."

Fred Astaire turns out to be a man who could do two things exceedingly well. He did a few other things reasonably well, too, including appearing in nondancing roles in a fair number of movies (among them *On the Beach*, *The Towering Inferno*, and the eminently dopey *The Amazing Dobermans*, et alia). He had his own radio show in the 1940s, and also appeared on several television shows: *The General Electric Theatre*, *Mr. Easy*, and *Fred Astaire's Alcoa Premier Theatre*, in which he presented television plays as the show's host and himself acted in five of these plays. Whether in comic or serious roles, he was a serviceable actor, okay, never an embarrassment, good even, but not good enough to be, as he invariably was on the dance floor, genuinely memorable.

No, of the two things Fred Astaire did supremely well, in the elevated sense that G. H. Hardy intends, dancing, obviously, was one. Dancers and choreographers from Balanchine to Nureyev to Gene Kelly all affirmed that as a dancer he was absolutely unsurpassable, the best ever. About this there doesn't seem to be much—any, really—argument.

But Astaire was also an extraordinarily fine singer. He was less a singer's singer—always, in some ways, an ambiguous compliment, suggesting that nonsingers don't really care all that much for your vocal performance—but that greater thing, a composer's singer. The Gershwins, Cole Porter, Jerome Kern, Dorothy Fields, Johnny Mercer, all wrote songs for Fred Astaire, and most went on record to say they took especial pleasure in doing so. "Astaire," Jerome Kern said, "*can't* do anything bad." Wilfred Sheed, in *The House That George Built*, his book about the great American composers of popular song, notes that it was Fred Astaire "who gave us the best of the new Kern, including the songs that people ask the cocktail pianists to sing most often, particularly 'The Way You Look Tonight,' but also 'I'm Old-Fashioned' and 'A Fine Romance.'"

At first George Gershwin was less than impressed with Astaire's voice, but he soon came to understand that no one interpreted his music in crisper, most pellucid fashion. Astaire said that George Gershwin "wrote for the feet," while Ira Gershwin wrote for the head. On his deathbed, the last word George Gershwin, who died at thirty-nine, was heard to utter was "Astaire."

Irving Berlin wrote songs with Fred Astaire specifically in mind, and was never disappointed in the result. "You gave Astaire a song," Berlin told the *New York Times* critic John S. Wilson, "and you could forget about it. He knew the song. He sang it the way you wrote it. He didn't change anything. And if he did change anything, he made it better. He might put a different emphasis on the lyric. He'd do things that you hoped other singers wouldn't do." The songs he wrote for the Astaire-Rogers movie

Top Hat, Irving Berlin claimed, were far and away his favorite of all the movie music he wrote. These included "No Strings," "Isn't This a Lovely Day," "Top Hat, White Tie, and Tails," "The Piccolino," and "Cheek to Cheek." Berlin extolled Astaire's range and his perfectionism. "He's not just a great dancer," Berlin said, "he's a great singer of songs. He's as good as any of them—as good as Jolson or Crosby or Sinatra. He's just as good a singer as he is a dancer—not necessarily because of his voice but by his conception of projecting a song."

Wilfred Sheed wrote that "it's as if Astaire's sense of the sounds he wanted and Berlin's sense of Fred's essence, his image, added up to a third personality, a city boy harnessed to a country boy in the cause of that magnificent anomaly, American sophistication." Sheed adds: "With Astaire everything is a rhythm number, love songs and all, so you get the whole Irving writing at once, the jester and the troubadour moving like quicksilver but in no special hurry, with the added bonus that Fred was always in fashion."

Much of Fred Astaire's best singing begins in the manner known as *parlando*, or talky. (Rex Harrison made excellent use of *parlando*, or simulating song in speech, in *My Fair Lady*, as did Richard Burton in *Camelot*.) Often when he begins a song Astaire seems to be talking, then elides into song, then slides back to talk, then song, talk, song. "They all laughed at Christopher Columbus, when he said the world was round" (talk). "They all laughed when Edison [elide into song] discovered sound." Then: "They laughed at me, loving you . . ." pure song.

People don't speak much these days about diction—diction in the sense of clear yet personally distinctive pronunciation. Once it was stressed in schools, as part of public speaking courses or, more old-fashioned still, as part of the art of elocution. Popular singers of the old school all had their own especial diction; it was often the fingerprint they left on the songs they sang. Sinatra had his, which came with a slight New Jersey twist; Bing Crosby had his, accompanied by a croony drawl; Peggy Lee had her southern lilt; Louis Armstrong had his rasp with a smile built into it; Fats Waller had his *basso ironico* (pardon the neologism and fake Italian), allowing him to mock the words of the song he was in the very act of singing (words he often wrote himself). Kenneth Tynan thought that Danny Kaye had the best diction of anyone among Anglophone singers and actors, which made it possible to understand every word he spoke or sang, no matter how fast or falsetto. My own candidate for the loveliest, purest diction of all would be that of Ella Fitzgerald.

Fred Astaire's diction was clarity itself, his phrasings perfection. Every word rings, every syllable sounds, every sentence sings. This Nebraska-born boy added a touch of eastern seaboard upper class to the proceedings: "Won't you change paadners and daance with me"; "after" often came out "aafter." He was the one, in the Gershwin song "Let's Call the Whole Thing Off," more likely to say "tomaato," "potaato," and "ersters" instead of tomato, potato, and oysters.

Standard descriptions of Astaire's singing voice include the words *reedy* and *wobbly*. Some said that his full vocal reach was only an octave, but if so, within that octave he could get an awful lot accomplished. His diction also enabled him to bend words nicely to the rhythms of songs, so that "umbrella" emerges as "um-ber-ella" with no harm done. And as he grew older his voice became richer, more mellow.

Astaire didn't sound quite like anyone else, yet if a comparison is needed, his voice perhaps resembles an urbane and more upper-class version of Hoagy Carmichael's. The voices of both men have something of the character of the nonprofessional, of the nonchalant, of someone just noodling at a piano keyboard, trying out a tune, slightly off-key sometimes, no big deal, then suddenly things pick up and the song sung becomes not merely charming but in their versions of it definitive: the right, the only, way the song should be sung.

Certain songs belong to certain singers—"Fever" to Peggy Lee, "It Was a Very Good Year" to Frank Sinatra, "Mack the Knife" to Bobby Darin—and everyone else does well not to attempt them. These singers in effect own those songs. Astaire owned more than his share of songs: "Cheek to Cheek," "Top Hat, White Tie, and Tails," "Change Partners," "Puttin' on the Ritz," "Dancing in the Dark," "Isn't This a Lovely Day," "Let's Call the Whole Thing Off," "They Can't Take That Away from Me," "The Way You Look Tonight," "A Fine Romance," and a number of others.

"Almost every great male icon of the art [of singing]— Crosby, Sinatra, Tormé, Bennett—takes from Astaire," the jazz critic Steve Schwartz writes. "The male pop singer B.F. (before Fred) sounded something like an Irish tenor. . . . The limitations of Astaire's voice forced him to find another way—deceptively casual, never oversold, and at home with the American vernacular. Astaire moved the 'scene' of the singer from the center of the great hall to just across the table, in effect replacing the Minstrel Boy with Ordinary Guy, U.S. version."

In Fred Astaire's singing as in his dancing, the aristocrat combines with the democrat in a winning way.

Schwartz adds: "One of the first things you notice about an Astaire song is its intimacy. Astaire didn't do all this by himself. Among other things, he benefited hugely from the development of microphone and recording technology. Others also contributed to a new definition of vernacular music—Louis Armstrong, Bessie Smith, Mildred Bailey, Billie Holiday, Nat Cole, to name a few—but Astaire essentially carved out his own territory: white male pop (as opposed to jazz) singing."

As a stage performer, Astaire sang a fairly large number of quite hopelessly junky songs, some of which he recycled for movies (such as "I Love Louisa," done in a stagy German accent and repeated in *The Band Wagon*), others of which he did only on the stage: wonderfully forgettable songs with such titles as "The Gold Digger's Son" and "Me and the Ghost Upstairs."

Only a small number of American songs are perfect. Even some otherwise lovely songs seem to have hopeless lines. "Under the hide of me, there's an old-fashioned yearning burning inside of me," for example, really needed Cole Porter to work a little harder to find a more elegant word than *hide;* and "When Fortune cries 'nay, nay' to me" is, mayn't we agree, less than Keatsian. "I've got a great big amount saved up in my love account" is a notably inane line Astaire had to sing; "Oh, I'm happy as a pup since love looked up at me" is another. Of "Drop your depression, have a yam session. Let's yam," let us not even speak.

But, then, all the great male vocalists seem to have had to sing a stupid song or two. Nat King Cole recorded a song about a family inventorying the contents of its hamper for a picnic that is embarrassing to listen to even when one is alone; "Dance, Ballerina, Dance" was no bargain either, though it doubtless made Nat Cole (and Vaughn Monroe, who also recorded it) lots of money. Sinatra, in *Pal Joey*, sang a couple of powerfully dud songs. "What a Wonderful World" ought to have been such a song, but Louis Armstrong, being a genius of a singer, made it seem damn fine.

In *American Popular Song*, Alec Wilder writes: "Every song written for Fred Astaire seems to bear his mark. Every writer, in my opinion, was vitalized by Astaire and wrote in a manner they had never quite written in before: he brought out in them something a little better than their best—a little more subtlety, flair, sophistication, wit, and style, qualities he himself possesses in generous measure." Wilder adds that Astaire "made listeners think lots of songs sound better than they really were," that "he could make 'Trees' sound good." Whitney Balliett wrote that Astaire "makes every song fresh and full-faced, as if each were important news." Bing Crosby said, "He has a remarkable ear for intonation, a great sense of rhythm and what is most important, he has great style—style in my way of thinking is a matter of delivery, phrasing, pace, emphasis, and most of all presence."

Fred Astaire wasn't so great that he could turn dross into musical gold, but swell songs written by first-class composers he always sang in a swell, first-class way. For the most part, he did best with songs that didn't suggest a roll in the hay soon to follow. He sensibly steered clear of heavy-breathing songs. Nor was he much with crudely dramatized songs, though he made "Bojangles of Harlem," a complicated song to sing, powerful and memorable. He was best with songs about couples trying to get back together, about patching things up, above all about getting back out on the dance floor. "The happiest men all got rhythm," as he says in a throwaway song. "Happiness is not a riddle/When I'm listenin' to that big bass fiddle."

"He's dancin' and he can't be bothered now." Dancing is therapy, philosophy, a way of life in the Astaire movies, and so it is in the Astaire songbook. Here is a partial list of songs he sang that touch on or are directly about dancing: "Cheek to Cheek," "Change Partners," "You're Easy to Dance With," "Dancing in the Dark," "I Won't Dance,"

"The Continental," "Let's Face the Music and Dance," "I'm Dancing and I Can't Be Bothered Now," "Bojangles of Harlem," "Shall We Dance," "The Piccolino," "I'd Rather Charleston," "The Shorty George," "Dig It," "The Yam," and "Never Gonna Dance."

In the songs he chose—and in most of those that in movies were chosen for him—the general byword was to keep things light. But in a few of his famous songs there is more than a hint of sensible hedonism brought on by philosophical pessimism. "Dancing in the Dark," for example, suggests that this is precisely what we're all doing in life, dancing in the dark, a version of whistling past the graveyard, "till the tune ends . . . and it soon ends . . . we're waltzing in the wonder of why we're here . . . time hurries by, we're here, and gone." And, in "I Concentrate on You," "whenever skies look gray" to him, "and troubles brew" or "whenever the blues become" his "only song" he concentrates on her. "Shall We Dance," yes, yes, better than giving in to despair, because "life is short, we're growing older," best not ever to be "an also-ran, so dance little lady, dance little man, dance whenever you can."

Purblind critics have suggested that, without his dancing, Fred Astaire would be of no further interest. When Astaire died, a writer in the *National Review* declared that

"Astaire the dancer transmogrified Astaire the singer, Astaire the lover, Astaire the actor, Astaire the comedian." Along with misusing the word *transmogrified*, whoever wrote this badly misstates the true case, which is that Fred Astaire's dancing infiltrated, informed, finally gave the tone and timbre to his singing. Listening to him sing, you await his breaking out into a dance. And, frequently, that is just what he does, tap shoes slapping the floor much as drumsticks do drums. His tap dancing was itself a species of musical instrument; his feet functioning as a one-man percussion section.

Astaire sang like a dancer. His clearly enunciated, strongly beat, often staccato rhythms were chiefly a dancer's rhythms; his syncopations, too, had lots of the dancer to them. This didn't mean that he couldn't bring considerable intimacy to a song. Oscar Levant thought Astaire "the best singer of songs the movie world ever knew. ... Presumably the runner up would be Bing Crosby, a wonderful fellow, though he doesn't have the unstressed elegance of Astaire."

The best way to hear Fred Astaire sing is not with the large orchestras that accompanied him in his movies but in something closer to a small-room or studio atmosphere. The finest of Astaire, recorded in the early 1950s, is found on the albums—now CDs—he did for Verve, with an all-star backup of jazz musicians that includes Oscar Peterson on piano, Ray Brown on bass, Charlie Shavers on trumpet, Barney Kessel on guitar, Alvin Stoller on drums, and Flip Phillips on tenor sax.

There is something ties-off, collar-open, long cigarette burning slowly in the ashtray, ice cubes tinkling in glasses in the background, something simultaneously hot and cool about the songs Fred Astaire did on these recordings. Jazz in its happier days—leave your deadly drugs at the door—is here on exhibition in its finest flowering. People with inside knowledge of these matters say that these albums were made without much rehearsal, and none required than more four takes. Charmingly insouciant they are, with the feeling of something tossed off, but only as true artists can toss something off, which is to say, after years of work.

Nat Hentoff said of Astaire's singing backed by these jazz musicians that it teaches "a lot about inner jazz rhythms." Syncopation came naturally to Astaire. He could play drums and piano; I have seen a photograph of him playing that most cumbersome of musical instruments, the accordion, which it seems unlikely even he could make appear elegant. He had had musical training, and knew songs, so to say, from the inside out. He himself composed songs, and though his songs never rang the gong of smashing hits, a few of them are quite singable, especially when sung by him: "I'm Building Up to an Awful Letdown" (with lyrics by Johnny Mercer) is a case most piquantly in point. But the songs Astaire sings on these Verve recordings, works revisited long after he had originally sung them in movies, have a sweet brilliance made possible by the high order of musicianship he and the ensemble he is working with bring to them. The version of "Night and Day" he sang in *The Gay Divorcee*, good as it is, doesn't hold a chandelier to the becalmed version he did in studio with these splendid jazz musicians.

A sure sign of a masterpiece in any field of art is the feeling we get, when listening to it, looking at it, or reading it, that this—and no other—is the way things should be done. When reading Henry James we feel that no one can do it better, until we read Tolstoy, when we feel the same thing; when watching a Balanchine ballet we feel that this is precisely the way it should be done until we watch a ballet choreographed by Petipa . . .

Listening to Fred Astaire, backed up by Oscar Peterson and Co., sing "Isn't This a Lovely Day," or "The Way You Look Tonight," one feels that if one could sing, this is exactly the way one would wish to be able to do it: pure, no frills, no engineering or jumped up arrangements, no show biz crapola—just a fellow with good diction and some miles on him singing fine songs the way they were meant to be sung. "I'm stepping out, my dear, to breathe an atmosphere that simply reeks with class, and I trust you'll excuse my dust, when I step on the gas." Schwoosh! Lovely, lovely, lovely!

Untoppable, really.

Dancing on Radio

Style, true style, always outlasts fashion, because style is finer, richer, deeper than fashion. Fashion is by its nature ephemeral; style, if it is genuine, pleases at all times. Fashion goes out of style, yet style never goes out of fashion.

A word of many meanings, *style*. For some people to be *in* fashion is to be *in* style. Some people use *style* to refer to attractive ornament, or flourishes of manner or dress—style, in this definition, is a matter merely of decoration. Art and literary historians often use the word to refer to the common qualities binding artistic productions of certain historical periods, such as Classical style, Baroque style, Rococo style, Romantic style, Postmodern style. Others are content to let the word express any-thing they admire or fancy: a suit, a handbag, or a wrist-watch is said, in this sense, to have style, or, to twist the word a bit, to be stylish.

True style runs deeper than all these meanings; it is a way of viewing the world—a way of viewing the world that at the same time exhibits a strong indication of what one thinks of the world. Easy enough to see how this sense of style might apply to a painter or anyone else working in the visual arts. Through their paintings, sculptures, buildings, designs, visual artists show us, fairly directly, how the world looks to them, or, possibly, how they wish it to look. In literature style tends to be repre-sented by point of view. Beneath the surface of the com-plex worlds of their fiction, Henry James, Joseph Con-rad, Marcel Proust, Edith Wharton, James Joyce, Willa Cather, and others reveal how they view the world—in its richness, variety, seriousness, comedy, darkness, gravity, and glory—and this view not merely informs but forms their styles.

Anyone who attempts to base his or her style largely on that of another artist or person makes a serious mistake. To have style is to be original. Style and originality are one: true style is originality, true originality is style. One can as soon copy another style, in the sense in which I have been describing it, as one can take over another person's precise way of looking at the world. One can try, I suppose, and even to some appearances succeed, but the result will be something very different from style and very far from originality.

Choreographers have style. George Balanchine had it, and so did Martha Graham, and so does Mark Morris, and so, too, does every other choreographer with any originality. One can see it everywhere in the formations of the dances they design, in the things they ask of their dancers' bodies, in the energy they infuse in the combinations of movement their dances require, in the rhythms that excite their imaginations.

But what about style for a dancer? "How can we know the dancer from the dance?" Yeats asked, and it's never been an easy question. In Fred Astaire's case it is made more complicated by the fact that Astaire choreographed many of his own dances; and even when he didn't, when Hermes Pan, or Michael Kidd, or some other Hollywood choreographer took the screen credit as choreographer, one has the feeling that, such was Astaire's fame and authority, in most instances the final word on how the dance was to be shaped was his. Even when under the sway of another's choreography, Astaire's style always left its own strong mark.

Not all Fred Astaire's dances for the movies, of which he did more than a hundred, were entirely successful. Owing to lapses in taste—sometimes his own, but more often those of other choreographers, or scriptwriters— he occasionally flubbed the dub: as in his comic dances with Betty Hutton, in his sad parody of early rock 'n' roll with Kay Thompson, in one or two of the numbers from *The Sky's the Limit*, and a few more. But overall his accomplishment was of a very high order, and all of these dances had his distinctive style stamped on them.

How does it come about that the great dancers and choreographers of the twentieth century all agreed on Fred Astaire's brilliance? Merce Cunningham, Margot Fonteyn, Rudolf Nureyev, Mikhail Baryshnikov, Jerome Robbins, George Balanchine did not hesitate to use the word *genius*, or words that, when brought together, spell out *genius*, when talking about Astaire's dancing. Even the great impresario of the Ballet Russe, Serge Diaghilev, according to John Mueller, was much impressed by Astaire's "charm and musicality." This is all the more notable when one comes to understand that dancers are not notably generous in their comments about fellow workers. When Ken Russell asked Nureyev to play the part of Nijinsky in a movie he was planning, Nureyev is supposed to have responded: "Why would I want to play the part of an inferior dancer?" Yet this same man called Astaire "the greatest dancer in American history." What did they all see when they saw Fred Astaire dance?

I suspect that they all saw a technique so assimilated to performance that it, technique, was all but invisible. They saw a man striving for perfection in what he did and coming very close to arriving at it.

After one has identified Fred Astaire's multiple and several steps and manifold moves—his swirling leaps, his twirling jumps, his slams, shuffling tap passages, spinning lifts, crazy-legged noodling, skips, hops, leg jabs, tap spins, struts, lunges, back kicks, tap barrages, high-stepping, stamping, darting, soft spins, arabesques, hip flips, saunterings, cross-overs, knee-and-pelvis jerks, strolls, turning jumps, steps done with a slight retard, syncopations, quick circling steps—after one has noted all these and the scores more of different moves he made, one still hasn't accounted for the magic in his performance. Can it be pinned down?

Astaire himself seemed to suggest that the attempt to do so wasn't worth it. "I don't know how it all started," he told an interviewer, "and I don't want to know." "I'm just a hoofer," he'd say. "I made a pretty good buck" was another of his standard retorts when people exclaimed over his genius. He did allow that he "did a great deal of listening and studying. I was pleased with lots of things but kept thinking of what I would like to try if I ever got in a position to make my own decisions."

The aesthetic behind the ballroom and tap dancing that Astaire did isn't always clear. His dancing has no central principle. Edwin Denby, who wrote about dance with greater clarity than anyone I've read, remarked that ballet was the art of balance: how simple a formulation and how splendidly explanatory! Read it and you understand at once that balance is essentially what ballet, both simple and elaborate, is about: delicate balance, gracious balance, floating balance, leaping balance, but always, in the end, balance. In a brilliant little essay, "Flight of the Dancer," Denby, after breaking down the constituent parts of the balletic leap, remarks that, while the dancer is in the air, "the shoulders have to be held rigidly down by main force, so they won't bob upward in the jump. The arms and neck, the hands and head have to look as comfortable and relaxed as if nothing were happening down below. Really there's as much going on down there as though the arms and head were picnicking on a volcano, but the upper half of the dancer's body must never show it. Brief but real calm is what she must show from the waist up." In other words, perfect balance.

But neither ballroom nor tap dance has principles of similar centrality. We might say that ballroom dancing should show fluidity, suavity, flair, above all a nice reciprocity of intimacy accompanied by elegantly disguised effort. Male and female created he them, the Bible says, and great ballroom dancers attempt, in their way, to show why. A subtle ballroom dance should hint at a story, preferably, perhaps obviously, a love story: passionate or joyous, a fantasy achieved. But unlike ballet or the more strenuous kinds of modern dance, ballroom dancing would seem to call for no special training. Unlike ballet and modern dance, everyone, presumably, can do it, with some people doing it a great deal more smoothly than others. But the problem for the professional ballroom dancer, for ballroom dance as entertainment, is how to do the basic steps and their variations without becoming excruciatingly boring to your audience.

In our day, ballroom dancing has become oddly professionalized and more than a mite goofy—a rich subject, in fact, for parody. Televised on PBS each year is a show called *America's Ballroom Challenge*, in which dancers (many of them dance instructors) compete in the categories of International Standard, American Smooth, American Rhythm, and Latin. The women who enter this competition tend to be dramatically romantic—and frankly sexy, as is emphasized by slashing gowns and towering heels—the men muscular with their hair pomaded to a high Valentino sheen. (The hairspray concession for these events would make one wealthy.) *Garish*, if not *vulgar*, is the word that best captures the entire spectacle of *America's Ballroom Challenge*. An amusing Australian movie called *Strictly Ballroom* scores many comic points on the artificiality of contemporary ballroom dance competition. But one of the things one quickly learns from watching these dancers is how quickly even the most highly dramatized ballroom dancing becomes dull. And they also remind one of how large was Astaire's achievement, while doing many of the same kinds of dances, in never coming close to boring.

Tap dancing, though more virtuosic and more often than not done alone, brings forth the same problem: how not to bore? How does one hold the interest of a crowd chiefly through the intricate and rhythmical slapping of one's feet upon the ground? The basic narrative of every tap dance is a crescendo of difficulty: the professional tap dance goes from the simple to the (all but) impossibly complex, ofttimes ending in exhaustion, preferably of the non-sweaty variety. What Fred Astaire was able to do was come up with endlessly different combinations within the confines of this rather strict narrative. Many of his tap routines spun around comic themes—drum bits, or empty shoes flying out of control, or tramps going uppity, or dancing while whacking golf balls off a tee; the underlying theme was solely joie de vivre, simple happy bloody joy in living. Sometimes he and his partner would break out of a ballroom dance and elide into a tap-dance duo, then return to ballroom or veer off into jitterbug. The physical delight of the dance was the thing, and to hell with the conscience of the king.

To bore, in show business, is to die. The audience must fall in the aisles, not drop off in their seats. "I have always tried," Astaire wrote in *Steps in Time*, "to carry out my steadfast rule of not repeating anything in dance that I've done before." Astaire worked and reworked his dance numbers, devising endless combinations, everywhere changing the alternations of steps, spinning off the tried and true, innovating wherever possible, keeping the ball in play, the game in action. He also knew how to take every dance up to the edge, teetering there, reaching beyond what seems to most the point of no return, riveting all our attention, and then landing oh so gently in the you-may-now-quite-justifiably-applaud posture.

Of course it wasn't the steps alone but how Astaire executed them, the special touch, twist, physical zing, and unflagging flair he gave to them. He did this through his choreographical skill, but he also did it by being Fred Astaire, by his style. Different dancers derive their power from various parts of their bodies. Leo Lerman, a balletomane of many years standing, thought that Baryshnikov's strength came from his perfectly shaped feet, Nureyev's from his buttocks, Edward Villella's from his thighs. Outside ballet, Gene Kelly's power derives from his muscular legs. But from where did Fred Astaire's power derive?

From his entire body: feet, arms, legs, torso, hands, all are brought into play in his dances. "Astaire sells body motion," the dancer Charles "Honi" Coles said, "not tap." "He's a *descriptive* dancer who works painstakingly with his musical accompaniment; he was the first to dance to programme music, describing every note in the dance," added Cholly Atkins. This is why Astaire's rehearsals were so long and arduous; every physical element, eyebrows, smile, the placement of a little finger, had to be in order, nothing could left to chance. He might combine balletic moves with ballroom ones, then beak into tap, out of which he emerges with jazz kicks and slides. He had to meet expectations while also surprising; predictability wasn't permitted.

Yet all the practice, all the care over the most minuscule of details, can produce only limited results if at the center of the enterprise great talent isn't there. The root and base of Fred Astaire's talent as a dancer (and as a singer) was an astonishing feeling for rhythm. In 1937 he did a radio show, *The Packard Hour,* in which he actually danced on radio, which entailed lots of machine-gun-like tapping. Dancing on the radio—it sounds like a joke, and is reminiscent of a bit Buster Keaton did in one of his movies, where, on a radio amateur hour, he juggles. In the movie the camera cuts away to people listening at home, twisting the dials on their radios, thinking there has been a disconnection, while Keaton solemnly juggles away down at the radio studio. But no one seemed to mind sitting home listening to Astaire dancing, picking up his wondrous, always varying beat on their old Philco radios.

Because Fred Astaire heard the music better than anyone else, he danced better to it than anyone else. Something similar has been said of George Balanchine, the choreographer, whose greatness is said to have come from his intimacy with, his living inside of, the music to which he choreographed his elegant or passionate or joyful dances. "George works from inside the music," said the composer Nicolas Nabokov. "He is the music." Balanchine, apparently, agreed, saying of Astaire that "He is terribly rare. He is like Bach, who in his time had a great concentration of ability, essence, knowledge, a spread of music. Astaire has that same concentration of genius; there is so much of the dance in him that it has been distilled." Obviously, it is not given to everyone to hear music so deeply, to know it in one's bones, but, as did George Balanchine, so, too, did Fred Astaire.

Think about the most heightened moment of any sport—the overhead smash in tennis, the home run in baseball, the running slam-dunk in basketball, the long, perfect putt in golf—Fred Astaire accomplished their equivalents, again and again and again, in his dances. Starting calmly, these dances rose to a succession of repeated smashes, slams, homers, perfect putts (*plunk!*). Did he gain the kind of pleasure out of these wonderful moves that athletes do from mastery over their own sports? From all one has heard about Astaire's insistence on more and more "takes" in the movies he danced in, my guess is, probably not. What he probably thought was he could do it a touch—ah, that decisive touch!—better next time.

Although he never used the word that I know of, Astaire was aiming for a pure elegance on the dance floor, in his movie persona, and in his life. Perhaps this is why lots of his comic dances, ingenious as many of them are, do not come up to his high standard. Comedy isn't elegant; quite the reverse, it is usually elegance falling on its duff. Elegance is polished, refined, graceful, poised, tasteful, urbane, restrained, precise, measured, never overdone. Some animals come by elegance naturally—cats, a small number of snakes, young horses, cantering giraffes—but no human being does. Men and women who desire elegance must work at it, cultivate it, hone themselves in preparation for it. And even after much work, elegance isn't available to everyone who seeks it. Fred Astaire sought it, and, most people would say, attained it to a very high power.

If his perfectionism prevented Fred Astaire from ever being quite happy in his achievement, he made those of us who watched him in his splendid cavortings extremely happy. Pure joy is what he gave to millions of people who saw his movies and the large numbers of people who continue to see them nowadays on television or DVD. It has been given to a small number of performers to make people feel happy in this way. Louis Armstrong is one; the young Judy Garland was another; Charlie Chaplin and Buster Keaton qualify; Ella Fitzgerald and Margot Fonteyn may be two others. A few more names could doubtless be adduced. But the number, in the end, will remain small.

Top Hat (1935) is often viewed as Fred Astaire at his zenith and thought to be the best movie he and Ginger Rogers made together. *Top Hat* was their fourth movie, and Astaire was much put off by the script. For one thing, it closely followed *The Gay Divorcee* as a movie revolving around mistaken identity; for another, he felt that the part he had to play was, as he put it, essentially that of "a *straight* juvenile & rather arrogant and cocky one at that—a sort of objectionable young man without charm or sympathy or humor." A tip on the weakness of the script, he felt, was that in not one but two scenes, Ginger Rogers slaps him. Something wrong there.

I cannot recall whether I've watched *Top Hat* five or six times, but I continue to find new little things in it. I discovered only on my last viewing what a perfect (I do not say good but perfect) singer Ginger Rogers could be for these Astaire-Rogers movies; she sang the way lots of young women might imagine themselves singing: in a voice warbly, thin, not in any way professional-sounding or overpowering but sweet, nice, pretty. One notices in *Top Hat*, too, that there isn't—apart from a young Lucille Ball, who appears fleetingly in a flower shop—a single person in the movie, apart from Astaire and Rogers, who isn't downright homely, if not slightly grotesque, thus lending the movie's two stars if not additional beauty at least added sheen. Dull as the script is, it is fearless in its references: at one point Ginger Rogers mentions Gertrude Stein, at another a black eye given to Edward Everett Horton is described by Astaire as resembling a Maxfield Parrish sunrise. Erik Rhodes, who plays a hopeless Italian clothes designer and Astaire's only and rather pathetic rival for Rogers, says to Horton, "You are in this plot. You are cahooting with him," which, as stage Italian goes, ain't bad.

Astaire was right: in this movie he does play a species of ninny, in this instance a well-off show-biz ninny named Jerry Travers. But this is the movie in which he sings what is perhaps his signature song: "Top Hat, White Tie, and Tails." He dances it solo, before a chorus of men also in top hat, white tie, and tails, whom he later shoots down, firing-squad fashion, with his walking stick. He and Ginger Rogers also do "Isn't This a Lovely Day," in a gazebo where they seek refuge from a heavy rain, and where they tap-dance facing each other in a way that is oddly affecting. In this movie, too, he and Rogers do "Cheek to Cheek," which, even with Rogers's notorious blue ostrich feathers from her dress flying about, is still a knockout. Astaire earlier does another solo, to "No Strings," which he does first in hard tap and then in soft shoe over sand, the second time to lull Dale Tremont (the Rogers character), in the hotel room below his, to sleep. Finally, they end with "The Piccolino," a song in the style of "The Carioca" (from *Flying Down to Rio*) and "The Continental" (from *The Gay Divorcee*), songs with large dancing choruses, and somewhat Busby Berkeleyan in their geometry and overhead camera work. The movie ends in an abbreviated dance version of "The Piccolino," with Astaire and Rogers, he in top hat and overcoat, she in gown and white fur, stepping out for a night in little ol' Venice—a super-energized hokey, yet somehow just right, ending.

Why does this nonsense charm? Part of the charm, surely, is in the perfect irrelevance of all that has gone on in the movie. Nothing more is at stake in this movie than getting Ginger Rogers straight about who Fred Astaire really is and isn't (he isn't, as she is led to believe, the husband of her dear friend, played by Helen Broderick), so that they might dance off together, which is precisely what, at the movie's end, they of course do. You have this pretty girl and this far from handsome yet smoothly attractive guy, and the two of them join together to dance like nobody else, before or since, and some terrific music is playing much of the time, so what the hell, but wouldn't it be great if life had more such moments: glamorous, romantic, elegant, yes, and uncomplicatedly happy.

Switch to a movie of 2007 called *Breaking and Entering*, with Jude Law and Juliette Binoche, set in London at the present time. Not a bad movie, *Breaking and Entering*, you won't be bored watching it, or think when it is over you wished you had instead done a couple of loads of laundry. But it contains an autistic child, a Russian prostitute, exiles from Bosnia who have turned into thieves, oral sex, and lots of rage. At the movie's end you do not leave the theater, or your couch, with a hop in your step or a song in your heart.

Of course, we don't have to choose between *Breaking and Entering* and *Top Hat*; we can watch both, on succeeding nights, or even one after the other. But why is the utterly frivolous *Top Hat* likely to stick in one's mind, and the serious *Breaking and Entering* to disappear into the clutter of one's already too clogged mental closet?

Because, I should say, that in *Top Hat* Fred Astaire provided certain utterly charming moments: his rendering, in voice and afoot, of "Top Hat, White Tie, and Tails," his soft-shoe number danced in sand, his and Ginger Rogers's whirling, swirling rendition of "Cheek to Cheek." These things stick in the mind; they are unforgettable. And they are so because they register grace notes, from a man who took the gift of his talent and through unrelenting hard work made to the rest of us a present of his art.

"He takes a job," the novelist John O'Hara wrote about Fred Astaire, "he works and works on it until he is ready, and then he delivers. And then he goes home. That is the magic formula, and anybody can do the same, provided he is endowed with the physical equipment of a decathlon champion, the imagination of an artist, the perseverance of an expert in dressage, the determination of a gyrene drill sergeant, the self-confidence of a lion tamer, the self-criticism of a neophyte in holy orders, the pride of a man who has created his own tradition."

Someone I know once said about a famous dance company that it tries to pass off what it does as art but it is really no more than entertainment. In the case of Fred Astaire, the reverse is often the case: what starts out to be entertainment ends up as art. I don't think Fred Astaire ever used the word *art* in connection with his own work, except to pooh-pooh it. He never thought of himself as other than an entertainer, and longed only to be the best entertainer it was in him to be. For him entertainment, with boos and applause and box-office figures, was real. Art was something else, an aspiration he never avowed, a pretense he never claimed.

And yet, as we have seen, nearly all the great figures in the art of dance claimed artistry of the highest caliber for Fred Astaire. How did this self-advertised hoofer, this ballroom dancer working in the tradition of low-grade acts with names like Maurice and Margo, attain to art? Through a natural talent, an uncanny rhythmic sense, an inexhaustible imagination for dance invention, and a fanatical devotion to polishing to near perfection all that he did. One form that genius sometimes takes is to transform one system into another—in Fred Astaire's case, the transformation was from entertainment into art.

He was not, I think, a genius. Schopenhauer, in his essay on genius, makes the necessary distinction between talent and genius. "Talent is like a marksman," he wrote, "who hits a target that the rest cannot reach; genius, one who hits a target they cannot even sight." Schopenhauer felt that "talent is able to achieve that which surpasses others' ability to perform, though not their ability to apprehend; it therefore immediately finds its appreciators." Astaire, in this definition or any other serious definition, was no genius. What he was, though, was immensely, charmingly, winningly talented, and what made him as great as he was is that no one worked harder than he to get the very most out of his talent.

An American artist Fred Astaire indubitably was, but does this make him, as in the title of the series in which this book appears, an *icon*? *Icon* is an old word given a new life through a new, possibly dubious meaning. Traditionally, of course, an icon is a small religious painting, often used for worship. Of the traditional definition, only the aspect of worship has been carried over into the word's contemporary meaning, a meaning that today has chiefly to do with celebrity. In this connection, an icon is someone or something that is celebrated with an intensity close, I suppose, to worship, or worthy of worship.

Once, in sports, in show business, even in plain business, there were people designated *stars*, a metaphor suggesting that they rose and shone above all others in their particular realms. Somehow the sky too rapidly filled with stars, and so *superstars* were called into play. Soon too many people were being called superstars, so something new and still grander was needed, and what it turned out to be was *icons*. When I began this book, I told a friend that it was to be part of a series on American Icons. "A nonsense word, *icon*," I said to my friend. "What do you mean, 'nonsense'?" he replied. "What about Ike and Tina Turner?"

What I take *icon* really to mean, then, is someone or something that has arrived at a level of renown bordering on the worshipful and that carries a weight of significance beyond mere celebrity or standard conceptions of fame. As for fame, the comedian Richard Pryor once defined it as having one's caricature recognized by everyone without needing a caption under it. Fred Astaire qualified here, and in most quarters—I am not sure about the very young, who may not know his name, though if they are interested in style they one day will know it—qualifies still.

What Fred Astaire did was elevate the entertainment of popular dance into an art; and he did it by dint of superior taste and sublime style, and while at it he also established that it was possible to bring a touch of the aristocrat to a thoroughly democratic society. He was an unconscious artist who regularly maintained the highest standard while appealing to the largest audiences. Do all that—and Fred Astaire did it all, and more—and I do believe you qualify as an icon.

Bibliographical Note

The amount of penetrating writing about Fred Astaire is less than overwhelming. The best book on him as a dancer, in my opinion, is John Mueller's *Astaire Dancing: The Musical Films* (1985). A slenderer volume, but no less acute, is Arlene Croce's *The Fred Astaire and Ginger Rogers Book* (1972). In *Fred Astaire* (1979) the English jazz critic Benny Green provides many useful observations, and is particularly good on the London portion of the careers of Fred and Adele Astaire. Most of the straight biographical literature on Astaire does not rise much above the level of fan magazines, though Tim Satchell's *Astaire: The Biography* (1987) does attempt to cut below the surface of its subject's success story to unearth a bit of dirt, especially about his subject's late-life marriage. Larry Billman's *Fred Astaire: A Bio-Bibliography* (1997) is invaluable for supplying reliable factual information on all of the dancer's stage, movie, and television performances. Sarah Giles's *Fred Astaire: His Friends Talk* (1988) is a pleasing compendium of comments on Astaire's life and dedication to his work by friends and colleagues, accompanied by splendid photographs. G. Bruce Foster's *Fred Astaire Style* (2004) is excellent on Astaire's clothes and the way he wore them. Finally, Astaire's autobiography *Steps in Time* (1959), though, like the man himself, laconic and sedulous in its avoidance of the painful in his personal life, is valuable if only because, unlike all other writing about Fred Astaire, it alone can answer affirmatively the question, "Vas ya dere, Charlie?"

Among the heavily illustrated books about Fred Astaire I consulted are those of Michael Freeland, Roy Pickard, and Stanley Green and Burt Goldblatt.

Fred Astaire plays more than a cameo part in Ginger Rogers's *Ginger: My Story* (1991). He shows up in David Niven's and other Hollywood memoirs, usually fleetingly, generally not saying much, there merely as an ornament, often in a glittering list along with other such magical names as those of Gary Cooper, Myrna Loy, Noël Coward, James Stewart, Irene Dunne, William Powell, Bing Crosby—in other words, the old Hollywood A list.

As of today, there is no definitive biography of Fred Astaire, one revealing that he led a secret life, devious, creepy, and dread-filled, and if the great dancer's luck holds out, there never will be.

Index of Names

Page numbers in **boldface** indicate illustrations